Digital Energetics

IN SEARCH OF MEDIA

Timon Beyes, Mercedes Bunz, and
Wendy Hui Kyong Chun, Series Editors

Digital Energetics

Anne Pasek, Cindy Kaiying Lin, Zane Griffin Talley Cooper, and Jordan B. Kinder

IN SEARCH OF MEDIA

University of Minnesota Press
Minneapolis
London

meson press

In Search of Media is a collaboration between the University
of Minnesota Press and meson press, an open access
publisher, https://meson.press.

Published by the University of Minnesota Press, 2023
111 Third Avenue South, Suite 290
Minneapolis, MN 55401-2520
https://www.upress.umn.edu

in collaboration with
meson press
Salzstrasse 1
21335 Lüneburg, Germany
https://meson.press

ISBN 978-1-5179-1587-2 (pb)
A Cataloging-in-Publication record for this book is available
from the Library of Congress.

Contents

Series Foreword

"Media determine our situation," Friedrich Kittler infamously wrote in his *Introduction to Gramophone, Film, Typewriter.* Although this dictum is certainly extreme—and media archaeology has been critiqued for being overly dramatic and focused on technological developments—it propels us to keep thinking about media as setting the terms for which we live, socialize, communicate, organize, do scholarship, et cetera. After all, as Kittler continued in his opening statement almost thirty years ago, our situation, "in spite or because" of media, "deserves a description." What, then, are the terms—the limits, the conditions, the periods, the relations, the phrases—of media? And, what is the relationship between these terms and determination? This book series, *In Search of Media,* answers these questions by investigating the often elliptical "terms of media" under which users operate. That is, rather than produce a series of explanatory keyword-based texts to describe media practices, the goal is to understand the conditions (the "terms") under which media is produced, as well as the ways in which media impacts and changes these terms.

Clearly, the rise of search engines has fostered the proliferation and predominance of keywords and terms. At the same time, it has changed the very nature of keywords, since now any word and pattern can become "key." Even further, it has transformed the very process of learning, since search presumes that, (a) with the right phrase, any question can be answered and (b) that the answers lie within the database. The truth, in other words, is "in there." The impact of search/media on knowledge, however, goes beyond search engines. Increasingly, disciplines—from sociology to economics, from the arts to literature—are in search of media as a way to revitalize their methods and objects of study. Our current media situation therefore seems to imply a new term, understood as temporal shifts of mediatic conditioning. Most broadly, then, this series asks: What are the terms or conditions of knowledge itself? To answer this question, each book features interventions by two (or more) authors, whose approach to a term—to begin with: *communication, pattern discrimination, markets, remain, machine, archives, organize, action at a distance, undoing networks*—diverges and converges in surprising ways. By pairing up scholars from North America and Europe, this series also advances media theory by obviating the proverbial "ten year gap" that exists across language barriers due to the vagaries of translation and local academic customs and in order to provoke new descriptions, prescriptions, and hypotheses—to rethink and reimagine what media can and must do.

Locating Digital Energetics

**Anne Pasek, Cindy Kaiying Lin,
Zane Griffin Talley Cooper, and Jordan B. Kinder**

Where is energy in media? And where are media in energy?

If—as etymology reminds—media studies is the study of middles,
then surely energy is itself a dynamic, differentiating kind of
middle. This condition is in part quite literal, especially when
considering the role of electricity in our digital present: energy is in
the middle of our devices, manipulating lights, powering circuits,
and vibrating airwaves. But this has always been the case, even
if energy was less visible in the production and consumption of
earlier media forms. Energy makes media function, whether in
the batteries of a smartphone or the metabolism of the worker
operating a printing press.

Yet energy is more than simply *in* media; it mediates. A more am-
bitious definition of energy in the capacity of media might take the
infrastructural view, showing how different energy regimes stand
in the structuring background of supply chains, the congealed labor
processes of commodity forms, and values and assumptions in
design—all predicated on certain kinds of fuels with concomitant
assumptions about how our structures of connection are assumed
to work (and so often do). This view of energetic mediation shows
how the technological and social configurations of manual or

steam-powered presses pull toward different potential ends: for workers, certainly, but also for the wider economic, environmental, and social worlds that media undergird.

Likewise, as thoroughfares between places, times, states, and forms, media make energy systems manipulable and knowable. Smart grids, calorie counters, cybernetic thermostats, and the Taylorist measurement of muscles on the assembly line are all interrelated examples of media systems that manage energetic work. If, as Prigogine and Stengers (1984, 117) argue, energy can be understood simply as the "function of the state of a system," then the work of energetic mediation concerns the measurement and manipulation of system states. One can then approach media as an integral part of the theorization and implementation of energy regimes—from the electric, thermal, informational, and metabolic.

To search for media in energy and energy in media is to set one's sights on excavating the often-obscured infrastructures and relations that fuel media ecologies, on one hand, and the ways we understand and relate to energy as a mediating force, on the other. This search has become all the more urgent in the face of ongoing and overlapping crises of work and climate, jointly propelled by the fossil-powered energy regimes in which our current media environments are imbricated. Better understanding the contours of energy in media and media in energy is essential to the task of dismantling these ties and configuring more just conditions for the workers, peoples, and ecosystems energy and media interconnect.

In this collection, we detail the directions and concerns of an "energy analytic" that serves as a conceptual bridge between media studies and the burgeoning field of the energy humanities. By "energy analytic," we frame both an argument about the world and a method of study. Across the histories and geographies of media, we observe how energy is frequently enrolled to mediate tensions between labor (that of workers and, increasingly, the social and affective networks through which data and value can be extracted) and materiality (of infrastructures, environments, and media itself), defining the terms through which our relations to wider communities, political economies, and ecologies are set. As a product, process, and idea, energy is caught in the middle of these sociotechnical systems, mobilized by actors seeking to renegotiate these arrangements from both above and below. Transforming these insights into method, an energy analytic aims to determine how tensions between these two fields are disrupted, redistributed, or deferred. A change in energy can speed up a production line, render certain types of production redundant, and move others offshore or into the home. At the same time, the physical externalities of energy, the apparent materiality of the commodity form, and the uneven geographies of its supply chains can all be mobilized to attract or refuse particular forms of social relations or to propose new forms of valuation. Our aim, therefore, is to follow energy into these arrangements, attentive to the struggles and investments tied to this dynamic and differentiating middle.

While an energy analytic can pay dividends across the diverse objects of media studies, we find it particularly urgent, in the midst of hotly contested economic and ecological transformations, to analyses of digital systems past and present. As such, in this book, we focus our collective efforts on tracing digital energetics from the chip to the grid and back. Our chapters are grounded in different overlapping methodological corners of media studies (information and management sciences, communication studies, assorted materialisms, and more humanistic tools of inquiry) and geographies (the United States, Iceland, Indonesia, and Canada). Our shared, animating hunch is that by figuring energy in media and energy as media in ways that account for differential scales and sites, we might be able to construct theories of the digital that are more adequately attuned to the shifting tensions between materiality and value. Digital operations are necessarily energetic, and, as a result, questions of computational work, expertise, geographies, and efficiencies have to be understood in relation to the histories and logics of energy cultures. At stake are not only sharper analyses of the digital economies and social forms of the present but our environmental and labor prospects for the future.

Energy in Media Studies

The ways energy has appeared in media theory inform how we might define and operationalize how energy mediates and is mediated. As yet, at least three major strategies are on the table.

In the first, scholars have approached energy as a site of aesthetic spectacle and political representation. Brian Larkin's (2008) study of Nigerian electrification remains a salient example, demonstrating how British authorities and their proxies invested capital and expectations in public lighting and radio as both a display and a mode of governing power. By cultivating and recounting moments of the "colonial sublime" (36) that emerged in the face of radically different sensory modes, new energy cultures proved to be an important, if contingent, site of political ritual (see also Schivelbusch 1988). Media, here, are a representational mode in which energy and its infrastructural orders are staged. Such stories of modernist disruption invite parallel attention to energy and aesthetic regimes that are more quotidian and hold more ambiguous ties to power. This can be found in contemporary literary and media analyses, through an orientation toward "resource aesthetics" (Bellamy, O'Driscoll, and Simpson 2016) and everyday energy epistemologies (Szeman and Boyer 2017, 6; Pasek 2020; LeMenager 2014) within the field of the energy humanities. In this work, media are sites for an extended Jamesonian analysis of the specific energy forms, expectations, and contradictions that structure both modern cultural production and wider economic relations.

A second school of thought can be found in studies of energy that, like many strands of North American and German media studies, are oriented toward the sociotechnical affordances and historical path dependencies at the root of a given medium. In this setting, Marshall McLuhan's (1994) famous remark about the lightbulb as a messageless medium (8) and his all-encompassing claims about

the collapse of spatial and sensorial orders in the face of new
(electronic) mass media (3–4) can be read as forerunners of more
granular media histories and genealogies. Doron Galili's (2020)
study of the prehistory of television, for example, provides an
account of the medium that is contoured by energy, arguing that
cinema's nonelectric antecedents bound it to a necessarily different
social and aesthetic trajectory than television's prefiguration in
histories of electric signal traffic. Against a determinism that is
inflected in much earlier scholarship, this kind of analysis largely
seeks to enroll energy into preexisting (if, at times, contradictory)
debates about medium specificity, the social construction of
technology, and media archaeology's emphasis on the paths only
partially taken. This all points to an exciting, if yet largely untrod-
den, horizon where Kittlerian analyses of storage, transmission,
and processing can be flexibly applied to the analysis of media and
energy systems alike.

A third, more recent tendency can be found in the rise of new
materialist and environmental media studies. Such analyses focus
on appeals to the physical foundations and aftermaths of media
systems, as well as questions of infrastructural and labor conditions that studies of media representation often overlook. Maxwell
and Miller's (2012, 9) emphasis on media as "environmental
participants" marks a significant break to this end, as does Jennifer
Gabrys's (2011, 2014) and Sean Cubitt's (2017) processual readings
of media systems. Scholars in this tradition are often led by a
provocatively "deflationary" orientation toward cultural production,
tempering expectations for the political potential of aesthetics with
the sobering insights of political ecology (Devine 2019, 169). While
e-waste, mining, and other toxic processes have held the lion's
share of attention in such studies, energy remains an important
and interconnected site of materialist attention, particularly in the
environmental, colonial, and racial histories of digital energy demand and storage (Riofrancos 2020; Bresnihan and Brodie 2020).

As these three tendencies demonstrate, energy is already a subject
and means of analysis within media studies at large, integrated into

long-standing methodological trajectories while helping to chart new ones. Yet, the breadth of these directions reveals evident tensions in the field and so poses new questions for consideration. For instance, should energy be approached primarily for its signifying affordances or its mediating potential (and are these tendencies always at odds)? Can fuel be taken as a given, sufficiently downstream from culture, or as a determinant, from the bottom of the social structure to the top? Any answer here further cuts across how we might define media in light of an energy analytic: Are our objects of study truly objects? Where do we begin to define the boundaries of such objects, and what do such cuts imply? Or, alternatively, are they best approached as a set of relations?

Media in Energy Theories

These tensions invite a reexamination of what the term *energy* entails. After all, energy, like media, is diffusely defined. Both concepts can refer variably to means of conveyance, aesthetic regimes, or social relations. These multiple and differentiating meanings are particularly apparent in the case of energy, where jumbled contextual uses and formations are roughly seamed together across the concrete and abstract. As such, it is analytically rewarding to distinguish between the different patchwork definitions of the word, not only to better comprehend the differentiating and at times contradictory tendencies that operate within our energy analytics but also to better denaturalize and parochialize how and what energy means in different contexts.

Per conventional dictionary definitions, energy can be approached as the ability to perform work. But what is work, and how do we make sense of its relationship to energy? In physics, shorn of context by mathematics, *work* is a rather loose term, encompassing all sorts of differentiations, from the pull of gravitational attraction to the splitting of the atom. It argues, simply put, that work is the transference of energy. This definition allows muscles and combustion engines to be jointly apprehended in joules of force expended, effecting a kind of posthuman commensuration between organic and inorganic forces. Signal processing and information theory, formally agnostic to the specific materializations of a given symbol, are inheritors of this tradition.

But this approach comes with freighted expectations to optimize more than just bits of data. Energy-as-work also produces distinctions between the productive and unproductive, with the latter conceptually parceled out as entropy. As Cara New Daggett (2019) details, the concept of energy-as-work finds its formation in Protestant industrialists of the nineteenth century, who were jointly concerned with moral and capitalist projects of efficiency, growth, and imperialist expansion. Energy became a way of endlessly increasing the horizons of work and so, too, the problems of "wasted" potential energy, whether it be in colonized populations, untrammeled landscapes, or coal left unburned in Newcastle mines (see also Rabinbach 1990). By focusing on the productive effects of work while remaining agnostic to the social and material character of that generative force (and the unavoidable losses incurred in its wake), energy-as-work is a conceptual move that depends on a retreat from material and cultural specificities.[1] Context-agnostic treatments of energy remain a contemporary hazard to professional and social accounts of energy systems: gaps to which an energy analytic must attend.

A more contemporary variation on this concept can be found today in the conflation of energy with fuel and electricity. We speak of energy bills, energy savings, and energy policy in similarly broad strokes, ignoring geographic and material differences. This approach cuts to the chase with its focus on the direct inputs of industrial and consumer devices yet still elides distinctions in the character of energy generation that lies farther up the power line. That such distinctions largely do not seem necessary is itself a product of modern petrocultures—that is, the habits and ways of life predicated on the abundance of both fossil energy sources and their ubiquitous distribution—at least in the Global North (Szeman and Boyer 2017; Wilson, Carlson, and Szeman 2017). The logistical advantages of oil, coal, and gas explain this absence of social attention: because fossil fuels can be transported, stored, and flexibly burned, they can easily provide uninterrupted coverage of contemporary energy needs and wants. Their ability to form deep stocks of energy reserves means that energy flows are constant, unremarked, and thus apt for conflation. Yet this tendency does not hold for renewable power; flows of solar and wind energy fluctuate with environmental variability and are not yet so easily captured and banked in batteries as fossil fuels. A fully decarbonized society would therefore be one in which the meaning of energy cannot be so agnostic to the character and consequence of different power sources. Attempts to fit greener energy systems into our current technical and social expectations of petrocultures thus obscure the larger challenges of an energy transition (Pinkus 2016, 5). Studies of energy cultures in the Global South, in varied hinterlands, and across the poverty line, conversely, reveal how the petrocultural ideal has never been universally achieved, even in contexts where it has been attempted, and so point to alternative political and creative strategies for attuning to flows over stocks. An energy analytic drawing from these insights will help rematerialize and politicize energy, in the social and spatial contexts in which energy regimes are built and contested.

A final definition of energy is one that is much more figurative and affective. Energy can describe the internal capacities of a subject, the subtle social character of an event, or the intensity of discourse in its utterance and circulation. When we speak of good or bad energy, that quality might variably belong to a space, a personality, a platform, or a ritual. It can be modulated through formal and relational aesthetics, by both perceiving and doing, or by the production and release of expectations. Energy, in these contexts, is communicative, social, and sometimes metaphysical. It binds together immanent, "animate circuits" (Stewart 2007, 3) of subjects and events, where our capacities are most legible in how we affect and are affected (Stewart 2007, 2). Other definitions of energy are often subtly entangled within this meaning, where work and fuel regimes may act as an important, if often ignored, backdrop to the

minor dramas and moods of contemporary life or as an intrusion
or instigator of new milieu. In adopting an affective dimension to its
concerns, energy analytics are rewarded with subtle but important
sites through which the social and technical dimensions of energy
systems come to matter.

An energy analytic, then, pursues the movement from energy to
energetics. Energetics, as the *Oxford English Dictionary (OED)* tells
us, describes both forces in the world and methods to describe
them—that is, "the branch of science concerned with the use,
transfer, loss, etc., of energy in physical, chemical, and biological
systems and processes" as well as "the properties of energy use,
transfer, loss, etc., within a system or process" themselves. Allan
Stoekl (2018, 22n2) extends these scientific definitions to the
broad remit of social theory, "to indicate an economic and social
structure based in a very specific type of energy use." Yet precisely
how scientific and mechanical formulations of energy move into
and contour our social, cultural, and communicative structures
demands explanation. Between Stoekl and the *OED,* energetics
provides a foundation and direction for our expansive understanding of energy and its relationship with our analytic task.

Through energetics, we argue that energy is never as simple as
blunt and brute work yet also never inextricable from it and so
must always be negotiated between contexts and through contes-
tations. Energy and media, in this way, become ways of organizing
and qualifying relations between entangled objects, processes,
and systems. These are frequently legible in the tensions between
materiality and labor: the ability to perform more or less work,
out of more or fewer resources, through a range of efforts and
elsewheres.

Digital Energetics

This book's conceptualization of energetics examines one particular junction between energy and media: the theoretical and
material articulations between contemporary, (largely) fossil-fueled

electrical systems and the logics and limits of digital devices and networks. From the switch to the chip, and from architecture to platform, data and energy are intertwined in ways that have yet to be fully explored—both within scholarly studies of the digital and in the climate trajectories of the information and communication technology sector more broadly. The book foregrounds how energy is central to the particular—and contested—epistemologies and logics embedded in digital technologies and cultures. We find it necessary in this historical moment marked by socioecological depletion to foreground the differential ways that the digital has inflected and enabled the ways we exploit, manipulate, centralize, contain, and mobilize energy.

In her opening chapter, Anne Pasek provides a survey of American computer history and present-day infrastructural politics, told through an energy analytic. By focalizing this history around the electron rather than the atom or the bit, she demonstrates an approach to digital media studies that can bridge both the perceived dematerialization of the personal computer revolution and the significant material externalities produced in its wake. This emphasis on circuits and electrons further reveals how energy efficiency—at first through external labor savings, and later internalized in energy and space improvements within both the chip and the data center—has been central to both the economic strategies of the sector and its recent environmental turn. Yet, as an analysis of the electrical and material architectures of digital systems reveals, the solution of energy efficiency is fast approaching its limits, forcing a new reckoning with energy stocks rather than flows.

In chapter 2, Zane Griffin Talley Cooper explores the materiality of the work in proof-of-work blockchain systems through a historical, sociopolitical, and energetic analysis of the heat managed in their antecedent infrastructures. By diving into the work in proof-of-work, and situating this work in the broader context of heat loss in digital systems, this chapter excavates a media archaeology of computational heat to build more robust vocabularies for how to think and talk about that which escapes through the cracks of media infrastructures. Through this lens of heat loss, Cooper frames proof-of-work systems not as exceptions but as profoundly visible representations of data infrastructures and their energy use more generally, arguing that these systems are uniquely salient case studies for interrogating long-standing assumptions about the fundamental relationships between data and energy and what these assumptions both conceal and reveal about the infrastructural futures of computing. This story begins at the site of an explosion, then follows the elastic concept of entropy and its entanglement with ideas of work from its roots in thermodynamic science through its permeation of information theory and to its centrality in proof-of-work ideologies. The chapter concludes with a call to use heat, and its many conceptual travelers, as a way to think through loss, waste, and externality in computing.

In chapter 3, Cindy Kaiying Lin unpacks how the logics of efficiency in database design so crucial for the software industry to prosper in northern California have been readapted to the energy constraints, social hierarchies, and norms of productivity installed in Indonesian governance. She elaborates on a yearlong attempt by Indonesian state computer engineers to build a high-performance computing storage system for satellite imagery data sets, a challenge that has also been undertaken by American tech corporations eager to maximize the potential and use of their cloud computing infrastructures in the Global South. At the heart of the chapter is how energy cultures in the West, which focus on managerial control and productivity of programmers, are subverted by engineers in Indonesia, who show how big data infrastructures can also be small, that efficiency doesn't necessarily instill managerial hierarchy, and that electrical and network constraints can bolster autonomy from corporate-owned cloud computing infrastructures.

Jordan B. Kinder closes the book by turning to a popular political engagement platform, NationBuilder, to address the ways in which digital platforms are imbricated in extractive, colonial energy regimes and simultaneously participate in shaping cultural imaginaries that inform these regimes. Proposing the term *platform*

12   *energetics* to describe this joint articulation between materials and cultures, he engages and expands on contemporary notions of data colonialism to link the concept more directly to how data colonialism—materially represented in the expansionary character of building new infrastructure to fuel the cloud—remains motivated by pursuits of land and territory. An environmental media studies that is becoming increasingly aware of the unsustainable character of the cloud-based present would do well to consider how questions of transition so pertinent to the energy and environmental humanities might apply to media environments. Kinder ultimately argues that through platform energetics, we can confront and work toward moving beyond the entanglement of platform, extractive, and fossil capitalism.

Together these chapters offer several directions for future media theories of energy and energy theories of media. We argue for an approach to history grounded in material commitments and consequences, while also offering a calculated return to theories of media specificity. We ask others to join us in focusing on energetic work, both in its displacements of historic workforces and materials and also in its reorganization of how bodies relate to impersonal machines and ever-more-personalized publics. An energy analytic of digital media shows how data technologies and infrastructures reconfigure what counts as labor while tracing the perseverance and discontinuities of dominant logics of energy across contexts. Our analytic also foregrounds how new political movements and resistances against (and for) forces of oppression and colonialism are mediated through digital energetics. We offer a call to follow the conceptual and material paths of energy through media to diverse and differing destinations, challenging the telos of energy's place in media and media's place in energy.

Note

1   See also Arendt's (1958) argument that industrialization has served to erode the distinction between labor (the futile but necessary efforts of [social] reproduction) and work (the conceptualization and production of durable goods with

both world-making and humanizing effects). To confuse our terms here, we can see the development of energy-as-work as a parallel and interrelated part of the shift to work-as-labor.

References

Arendt, Hannah. 1958. *The Human Condition.* Chicago: University of Chicago Press.

Bellamy, Brent Ryan, Michael O'Driscoll, and Mark Simpson. 2016. "Introduction: Toward a Theory of Resource Aesthetics." *Postmodern Culture* 26, no. 2. https://doi.org/10.1353/pmc.2016.0010.

Bresnihan, Patrick, and Patrick Brodie. 2020. "New Extractive Frontiers in Ireland and the Moebius Strip of Wind/Data." *Environment and Planning E: Nature and Space* 4, no. 4. https://doi.org/10.1177/2514848620970121.

Cubitt, Sean. 2017. *Finite Media: Environmental Implications of Digital Technologies.* Durham, N.C.: Duke University Press.

Daggett, Cara New. 2019. *The Birth of Energy: Fossil Fuels, Thermodynamics, and the Politics of Work.* Durham, N.C.: Duke University Press.

Devine, Kyle. 2019. *Decomposed: The Political Ecology of Music.* Cambridge, Mass.: MIT Press.

"energetics, n." *OED Online.* Oxford University Press. http://www.oed.com/view/Entry/57065387.

Gabrys, Jennifer. 2011. *Digital Rubbish: A Natural History of Electronics.* Ann Arbor: University of Michigan Press.

Gabrys, Jennifer. 2014. "Powering the Digital: From Energy Ecologies to Electronic Environmentalism." In *Media and the Ecological Crisis,* edited by Richard Maxwell, Jon Raundalen, and Nina Lager Vestberg, 3–18. New York: Taylor and Francis.

Galili, Doron. 2020. *Seeing by Electricity: The Emergence of Television, 1878–1939.* Durham, N.C.: Duke University Press.

Larkin, Brian. 2008. *Signal and Noise: Media, Infrastructure, and Urban Culture in Nigeria.* Durham, N.C.: Duke University Press.

LeMenager, Stephanie. 2014. *Living Oil: Petroleum Culture in the American Century.* New York: Oxford University Press.

Maxwell, Richard, and Toby Miller. 2012. *Greening the Media.* New York: Oxford University Press.

McLuhan, Marshall. 1994. *Understanding Media: The Extensions of Man.* Cambridge, Mass.: MIT Press.

Pasek, Anne. 2020. "Everyday Oil: Energy Infrastructures and Places That Have Yet to Become Strange." *Heliotrope,* September 14. https://www.heliotropejournal.net/helio/everyday-oil.

Pinkus, Karen. 2016. *Fuel: A Speculative Dictionary.* Minneapolis: University of Minnesota Press.

Rabinbach, Anson. 1990. *The Human Motor: Energy, Fatigue, and the Origins of Modernity.* New York: Basic Books.

Prigogine, Ilya, and Isabelle Stengers. 1984. *Order Out of Chaos: Man's New Dialogue with Nature.* New York: Bantam Books.

14   Riofrancos, Thea. 2020. *Resource Radicals: From Petro-nationalism to Post-extractivism in Ecuador.* Durham, N.C.: Duke University Press.

Schivelbusch, Wolfgang. 1995. *Disenchanted Night: The Industrialization of Light in the Nineteenth Century.* Berkeley: University of California Press.

Stewart, Kathleen. 2007. *Ordinary Affects.* Durham, N.C.: Duke University Press.

Stoekl, Allan. 2018. "Marxism, Materialism, and the Critique of Energy." In *Materialism and the Critique of Energy,* edited by Brent Ryan Bellamy and Jeff Diamanti, 1–26. Chicago, Ill.: MCM'.

Szeman, Imre, and Dominic Boyer. 2017. "Introduction: On the Energy Humanities." In *Energy Humanities: An Anthology,* edited by Imre Szeman and Dominic Boyer. Baltimore: Johns Hopkins University Press.

Wilson, Sheena, Adam Carlson, and Imre Szeman, eds. 2017. *Petrocultures: Oil, Politics, Culture.* Montreal, QC: McGill-Queen's University Press.

1

From Atoms to Electrons: An Energy History and Future of Computing

Anne Pasek

Few lines of digital media theory have attracted more corrective attention than Nicholas Negroponte's (1995) famous remark that the turn to a more digital society was, in essence, a transformation from the atom to the bit. With exponential speed, digitized goods and communications would supposedly undo conventional material limits on transportation and exchange, catalyzing a revolution not only in information but in culture, subjectivity, and political economy. Information would be everywhere, instantaneously and with minimal clutter—"the digital planet will look and feel like the head of a pin" (6).

This is a supposition that has proven to be as remarkably predictive in its general contours as it is shortsighted in its analysis of the material infrastructures required to make all this stuff seemingly disappear into the digital ether. The lived experience of the past decades has involved the retreat of newsprint, retail, and bulky desktops with a parallel acceleration of news cycles, global interconnections, and processing power. For the Global North user, dematerialization was palpable. But Negroponte was fundamentally wrong about atoms; we paradoxically depend on a huge and expanding number of distant resources and workers to deliver bits to ever-smaller digital devices.

This is a very well-worn line in my subfield of environmental media studies. We spend considerable time writing about the mines, toxic tailings, e-waste, and carbon emissions that stand behind the prodigious rise of digital cultures. Our much repeated refrain: the digital is not immaterial, the cloud is a factory, and the study of digital devices and economies requires a spatial and labor analysis of the convoluted supply chains that produce digital systems and their considerable environmental externalities (Ensmenger and Slayton 2017; Parikka 2015; Maxwell and Miller 2012).

Yet all refrains, even good ones, grow tiring over time. I sometimes find myself wondering at the conceptual limits of this emphatic rematerialization of digital media studies. In doing so, I do not want to discount the necessity of such corrections historically, or even today; the idea of digital dematerialization overlooks the racially differentiated health, environment, and climate legacies of the industry and confounds public policies that might better mitigate these hazards (Park and Pellow 2004; Hogan 2015). The repetition of this point continues to be evidently needed. But I worry that its seeming sufficiency risks boxing in this line of scholarship. At its best, a turn to the atom grounds our analysis in the stakes and ethics of labor and environmental struggles, using the material as an orientating device to think around overly abstract or user-centric accounts of the digital. At its worst, this tendency risks boxing the researcher into the role of clearinghouse distributor of more empirical findings from other fields—trafficking more in facts than analysis. And so, in addition to these materialist correctives, I find myself longing for more novel concepts.

As an experiment, I've returned to Negroponte's formula in a somewhat stubborn attempt to read it, if not generously, then at least differently. He did name and describe a real transformation in social life, even if he contributed to an inaccurate popular imaginary about its environmental implications. A more nuanced history

of the rise and future of computing might therefore strive to hold
both its radical phenomenological disruptions and banal repeti-
tions of industrial harms together in hand. We could ask, in parallel
to all the continuities we can draw between digital production and
older industrial forms, where, too, can we mark useful, distinct
breaks? And if atoms and bits are the wrong foils to describe this
shift, what might be a better synecdoche for digitization?

One promising direction lies within the material culture of
computing. A focus on the technical designs and lived experiences
of digital systems helps demonstrate how matter and data have
been jointly apprehended and obfuscated in popular metaphors
and objects alike (Chun 2006; Kittler 1999). As historians of science
argue, the models we build about the world emerge through the
material idiosyncrasies of the objects we have on hand to think
with (Pickering 1995, 16); these objects in turn leave us with specific
"possible technocultural moves" in their wake (Galison 2000, 389).
Getting closer to the material foundations of digital operations
might, paradoxically, help us better apprehend and critique the
seeming dematerialization of digital media.

So here is my gambit: what happens if we reexamine the history
of digital media as a partial shift from the atom to the electron?[1]
This chapter runs with the idea in many directions. I argue that an
energy analytic is more accurate to both the physical operations of
computer chips and the specificity of digital media more broadly;
electrical circuits were the objects around which the foundational
designs and expectations for the digital were formed and inflected.
What's more, the turn to electricity as a medium of computation
was also essential to the industry's prodigious growth, guided
by automation and the unique properties of Moore's law (which
remains to a significant degree a question of energy draw). I show
how this energy orientation repeats across the tech sector at
large—that the formal characteristics of microelectronics have
guided the macro-level build-out of data centers and the climate
trajectories of what are now among the largest companies on
earth today.

What follows is a necessarily brief and hasty history of American computing, told with an electrical slant. By way of method, it combines a Kittlerian emphasis on the materialities of engineering and design with a political economy approach attentive to the effects of these design considerations on the movements of capital. Across these analytic orientations, energy efficiency emerges as both a resource and a strategy: a technocultural move that casts a long shadow across digital conjunctures past and present. At first, these efficiencies were ones of industrial time and labor: the stocks and flows of feminized technical workers, their wages, and their work processes. Electrical alternatives to hands, gears, and paper achieved greater feats of speed and economy, automating these workers out of a job by doing more with less atoms. Yet, after the work of computation was digitized and electrified, electricity itself became a new kind of resource (and resource problem). More efficient flows of electrons enabled the industry to grow exponentially, though at the cost of ballooning aggregate energy demand.

This partial dematerialization-through-efficiency created two urgent problems for the information and communications technology (ICT) sector. First, as the energy to power the work of computation is increasingly provided by the industry itself in the form of large-scale data centers, rather than in consumer homes and businesses, the logistical challenges of moving ever more electrons loom large. Second, as the climate impacts of the sector come into greater scrutiny, and as the future growth or decline of its overall electrical demand is subject to increasing debate and uncertainty, the corporate and carbon budgets of ICT increasingly pose problems that efficiency may not be able to fix. Efficiency, in other words, deferred but did not resolve the issue of stocks and flows that the industry confronted in its infancy.

By grounding our analysis in the electron, environmental media studies can better trouble the meaning and scope of digital materiality. Beyond corrective and demonstrative appeals to the atom, we might be able to better explain how data, electricity, and labor came to be jointly articulated, what kinds of problems

and solutions this articulation makes legible at the corporate and
sectoral levels, and the kinds of alternative frames and directions
that are needed from below.

An Early Energy History of the Bit

Let's begin by troubling our terms: digital operations need not be
electric. Digital systems are simply any signaling system based
on discrete, binary values. Zeros and ones can be encoded in the
warp and weft of a loom (Plant 1997, 305), billiard balls (Fredkin
and Toffoli 1982), slime (Adamatzky and Schubert 2014), or a truly
improbable number of crabs (Gunji, Nishiyama, and Adamatsky
2011).[2]

It was only in the middle of the twentieth century that electricity
became consequential to computation. Prior to this, calculative
machines were composed of a diverse range of physical substrates,
including gears, film, and cards. These operations were sometimes
digital, sometimes analog; the distinction wasn't important to
practitioners in the same way that it is today (Kline 2019, 20).
Electricity was an input to such systems but not an essential part;
mechanized drums, belts, and cogs were powered by external
sources like any other manufacturing process. As such, rates of
calculation were limited by the movement and maintenance of
these interlocking parts. A reserve pool of increasingly feminized
labor—both calculative and clerical—provided a sometimes alternative, sometimes supplement to such devices and were largely
comparable in speed and precision through the 1930s and 1940s
(Light 1999, 460). In either respect, whether in arms and hands or
mechanical belts and gears, computation worked at a perceptible
pace because it was so contingent on human-scaled operations
(especially when computers were literally women).

Electrons, however, promised a faster and potentially leaner model
of production. Back in 1890, Herman Hollerith's tabulating machine
had made short work of the American census by using electrically
conductive wires to read data in punched cards. It delivered results

both early and under budget, leading to both the introduction of commercial information processing machines and the loss of thousands of data entry jobs in the census bureau. Yet this technology was primarily inscriptive, counting but not manipulating data. The calculative work that would define the basis of digital computation first required the formalization of algorithmic code and symbolic logic. In so doing, electricity would shift from being an input to being a medium of calculation.

Claude Shannon's ([1937] 1940) famous master's thesis was a part of this leap; as such, so was his material milieu. As a research assistant working with MIT's differential analyzer and as a summer student at Bell Labs, Shannon was immersed in an immense number of electromechanical relay switches (Guizzo 2003, 11). These served to control the connection of interlinked circuits, the operations of the differential analyzer's analog outputs, and the routing of calls and electricity through the telephone system. However, the design and legibility of switching systems were frequently idiosyncratic and poorly documented, posing problems to the newcomer and potentially the more fundamental operational efficiency of the system. Shannon's thesis begins by placing its reader in such a tangle of wire: if confronted by a mass of relays, how would you go about determining which circuit does what, and with what interlinked dependencies? The approaches that were most ready to hand involved either laboriously testing all the possible configurations of open and closed relays or (perhaps equally as arduously) working backward from the practical function of the system to inventory and then map the minimal circuitry requirements needed to solve the design problem (requirements which may or may not demonstrate the skeleton of the actually existing wires and relays) (Shannon [1937] 1940).

Shannon's alternative was to reach for a further layer of abstraction, moving from material engineering to symbolic logic and back again. By representing circuits as mathematical equations, he argued, system functions could be better mapped and inefficiencies identified. Given that a well-designed circuit will have only

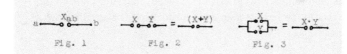

[Figure 1.1]. Diagrams of a basic circuit and its manipulation to show addition and multiplication functions. From Shannon ([1937] 1940, 5).

two baseline conditions (on or off—partially energized circuits are a hazard), a binary system of 0s and 1s or true/false statements could be readily applied to electrical systems and subsequently mapped to the symbolic logic of Boolean operations (Figure 1.1). Circuit relay analysis could thus be a kind of algebra, and vice versa. Moreover, once materialized in mathematically mapped wires and relays, "any operation that can be completely described to the required accuracy . . . can be done automatically" (Shannon [1937] 1940, 51). Unlike human computers, electrical mathematics could be practically instantaneous.

Perhaps we don't linger long enough in the fact that digital programming developed from the material culture of electrical engineering. Digital media studies generally omits an understanding of the circuit, focusing instead on underlying mathematical logics or the plasticity of data as the defining features of the systems it seeks to study. Yet circuits are at the material core of how such systems are built and executed; electricity is the medium of virtually all computational work today. So, let us be rather material for a moment, to assess both the historical trajectory of digital systems and the conceptual models inherited thereby.

A bit of remedial electronics may be useful to this end. A circuit is formed whenever an unbroken path of conductive material (most commonly wire) is joined to the positive and negative ends of an energy source. This causes electrons to rapidly circulate across the atoms of the conductor (typically the metal of the wire). This circuit becomes "electronic" when one or more active components are added to selectively interrupt or modulate this flow. The most basic of such components is a switch: a means to connect and disconnect the conductor's path and thus to break or seam the flow of electrons.

Flow is now a widely used concept in wider claims about globalization, network societies, and digital cultural more broadly. A more electronic definition adds some useful specificity to the concept. Electricity is the flow of electrons: a subatomic particle typically imagined in a kind of orbit around the much heavier nucleus, which exerts a balanced positive force to the electron's negative charge. As the outermost part of the atom, electrons are capable of jumping from the farthest orbits of one atom to the next. Some materials, like copper or the treated silicon of semiconductors, are composed of atoms with electron orbits that are particularly receptive to these kinds of leaps. This movement frees up space in the recently departed atom, which, owing to the shifting charge, attracts electrons in neighboring atoms to fill the vacancy. This creates a propagating flow, initiated and sustained by differences in electrical charge on either end of the conductive medium.[3]

Electrical current makes for a very useful medium of computation because it is so fast: in a circuit with a copper wire, electrons flow through atoms at a rate of three hundred million meters per second. This is possible because the rest of the atoms, with their much larger size and weight, remain relatively inert; it is only the outermost electron that moves. Friction and resistance still occur (primarily in the form of heat energy), yet to a far smaller degree than would be the case if the atomic whole were to move. This is by no means an immaterial process, but it is one that divides and orders matter very differently.

The advantages seem obvious: by shifting the media of computation from atoms to electrons, calculative work could be performed much faster and with programmed precision. A whig history of computation would therefore take for granted the immediate and obvious application of Shannon's thesis to industrial practice. Yet the reality is much murkier. On the telephone side of Shannon's milieu, the solution never quite matched the problem of call routing, as Boolean logic can't readily simulate temporal sequences. As such, the industry's engineers were fairly cool in their engagement with Shannon's ideas (Bullynck 2019, 92). Perhaps the need to demystify a tangle of wires wasn't so evident to the workers who connected them in the first place.

To management, however, the principle of automation was much more enticing. As an extension of the Taylorist drive to extract more work out of workers through projects of efficiency, and in response to growing worker compensation claims from the telephone industry's feminized switchboard workforce, electric action promised a usefully different kind of work. If electrons could perform at least some of the labor of these women, they might prevent expensive injuries, slow hiring demand, and thus improve the company's bottom line (Mills 2021). Electrical flows, in other words, could reduce capital stocks, at least where the workforce was concerned.

As for computers, this need to speed up calculative production and downsize its workforce only became acute in the context of the Second World War and its acceleration of complex ballistic and nuclear science. Atoms had to be split, both in the construction of new and devastating armaments and in the calculative labor processes required thereby. The world's first electronic and programmable computer, the Electronic Numerical Integrator and Computer (ENIAC), was funded by the U.S. Army on the premise that it would reduce the labor and time constraints of this work. In a memo pitching the project, its considerable costs were justified through appeals to speed and economy. The memo notes that, although more skilled engineers would be required to build, run, and maintain the device, "the number of persons required to turn out the same amount of finished work should be appreciably less in the case of the electronic computer" (Mauchly 1982, 356).

Electrical efficiency in this early moment, then, was primarily a means to overtake the material demands of labor, both in wages and in the bodily pace and costs of technical work. Automated electronics were a new kind of capital stock: one that would produce faster and faster flows of informational work. The circuit became the bit because of the efficiency gains it offered.

Yet the efficiency on offer was always only partial, resolving some production pressures and creating new ones in its wake. After all, electricity only works as a functional medium for computation if certain conditions are met and maintained—foremost, that electrical flows are kept in steady supply. This is true of the basic operability of all hardwired electronics: they need externally generated electricity to work, and so a power outage is generally also a computer outage. Yet this also holds for the quality of the electricity supplied: voltage must be constantly maintained in very narrow ranges. Voltage describes the charge difference between two terminals in a circuit; it works akin to water pressure in a hose. More volts in a system can do more work, though an oversupply can strain the physical integrity of circuit materials. Within digital relays, if voltage drops even momentarily, circuits may not open and close as designed, leading to cascading problems in the sequential processing of data. On the other hand, surges in voltage can destroy components entirely.

Much of the difficulty in the shift from mechanical to electric computation stemmed from negotiating these problems of insufficient or excessive electrical potential. The ENIAC, for example, was constructed with off-the-shelf vacuum tubes adapted from the radio industry owing to wartime production constraints. However, engineers soon discovered that they would have to run these circuits at voltages significantly less than the manufacturer's parameters to reduce the number of blown fuses and filaments involved in daily operations, given the propensity for surges across the system (Randall 2006). This required modulating the current through a host of transformers and resistors to meet the seventy-eight different voltages used throughout the computer. The ENIAC was in this sense a terribly inefficient machine: the energy used to perform work in the machine was significantly smaller than its total draw.

Second, electricity only works as a medium of computation if the ordered flow of electrons is not disrupted by noise in the environment. This kind of problem is not, in itself, unique to electrically processed signals, but the nature of electricity adds specific and recurring problems because, in addition to the hazards of disrupted flow from the power source, electricity is an ambient and variable factor. As anyone who has assembled a PC will know, static electricity needs to be carefully cordoned away from digital components for fear of accidentally shorting a circuit. Digital systems must therefore be insulated from wider environments at the scale of both the chassis and ground wires of individual machines and the geographical and social isolation of data centers and the many nonillions of transistors they house (Starosielski 2015, 19; Johnson 2019). Voltages must additionally be kept at higher levels than strictly needed for day-to-day operations because cosmic rays can periodically interfere with low-power electronics, flipping a circuit position and degrading the signal chain (Blanchette 2011, 1047). Heat, too, is a variable that must be bracketed out of the system, whether it originates within the electrical resistance of the circuit itself or in the local climate.[4] At all scales, electrical systems require overbuilding.

Given these factors, computation seemed set to be a very electrically intensive business. Indeed, the ENIAC was an industrial-scale machine, requiring its own air-conditioning system to prevent it from melting its components. It consumed 150–175 kilowatts of electricity when running (the equivalent draw of more than 120 American homes today). This scale was so remarkable that it inspired the rumor that, whenever the machine was switched on, lights across Philadelphia would momentarily dim as the electrical grid struggled to shoulder the load (Randall 2006). In fact, the computer was built with its own special direct-current power line, running through a generator, to protect its circuits from the variability of the municipal grid (War Department 1946). Grid power drove a motor, which in turn powered the machine, such that the mechanical inertia in the motor would even out fluctuations from the power line. Moreover, the whole assemblage was rarely turned off, as the thermal and material stress of warming up and cooling down the device's vacuum tubes produced parts failures. The ENIAC was thus an expensive and energy-intensive system—efficient in speed, but in very little else. As such, the future of computing looked to be restricted to large institutions capable of huge capital investments—those with ample budgets, space, power, and engineers.

Exponential Efficiencies, Exponential Growth

Yet the pursuit of efficiency would soon be directed inward. A pivotal turn to this end came in the shift from circuits borrowed from other industries to the design of integrated circuits and transistors designed specifically for computation and printed on silicon wafers. This move was again motivated by military demand: this time for chips and sensors small enough to fit into a burgeoning fleet of Cold War missile stocks. Civilian researchers and businesses were more or less content with ENIAC-sized machines; the pull of miniaturization was not self-evident (Noyce 1977, 64). Nevertheless, the call to produce more computational power out of fewer atoms did have the unintended consequence of revolutionizing the whole industry through the "discovery" of Moore's law and its unusual electromaterial logics.

Moore's law is not a physical law but is rather an observation about industry trends and the specific material properties of silicon. Coined by Gordan Moore in 1965, it states that the number of components on the most economically viable integrated circuit that the industry could make would double every year, thereby exponentially increasing processing power and cost savings per chip. Computers could therefore do more with less and so would get cheaper and more powerful in equal measure. In 1975, this prediction was later revised to describe doubling every two years. It has held true for an impressive number of decades.

Moore's law fundamentally describes the win-win of miniaturization and economies of scale. Unlike mechanical circuits, electrical flows in silicon are not wired but engraved into impeccably clean wafers with photosensitive treatments. As such, the same surface area of silicon can produce greater or lesser numbers of components, depending on the scale of the photoengraving process; chips do not so much need to be mechanically assembled as they need to be projected in light—another departure from the strict domain of the atom. Importantly, this affords a legible path toward exponential gains in density. These manufacturing advances had the effect of making each generation of chips much less expensive (more chips could be cut from the same materials, with the cost per area of processed silicon remaining constant; Mack 2011, 204), urging on greater applications of digital computing at a widening range of price points and sizes. As a result of this trend, mass-manufactured computer chips today are often composed of transistors less than fifteen nanometers wide, made of a total of fewer than fifty atoms. This is a truly remarkable feat—one that seems almost capable of making Negroponte's metaphor a reality.

Yet Moore's law is also, to a degree much less widely discussed, a question of electrical efficiency. Ever-smaller transistors meant that electrons would have increasingly limited distances to traverse and so such systems would need less and less voltage overall to operate. This has, in turn, inspired another descriptive "law," Koomey's law, which holds that the energy efficiency of digital devices operating at peak performance will double every one and a half years, outpacing even transistor density in its rate of exponential growth. A graph of calculations per kilowatt-hour, in other words, is a steady, upward line. The scale of this aggregate progress is hard to fathom; between 1940 and 2000, the energy efficiency of average peak performance improved by a factor of more than ten billion (Naffzinger and Koomey 2016).

These gains are a side effect of the economic incentives of miniaturization, yet one with increasingly central importance to the business and personal experience of computing. The electrical efficiencies of miniaturization significantly buttressed the cost savings and processing power gains that are the more legible outcomes of

Moore's law—commensurately shrinking energy needs made the exponential growth of digital systems viable at a practical level. And so enterprise machines that once filled entire rooms could be transformed into desktops, laptops, and then battery-powered, mobile devices, effecting a qualified sort of dematerialization. In the phenomenological world in which computation was lived, digital goods regularly shrank while still offering the same, if not better, processing power—fewer atoms, certainly on the user side of things.

Moore's law and Koomey's law have thus built an industry with expectations for exponential growth built into its foundations. Quick and steady gains via innovative efficiencies was at first a socioeconomic trend that became prediction, then eventually an assumed fact about the world at large, conditioning the techno-cultural moves that are commonly perceived within the penumbra of the digital. This is true within ICT, in the road maps established by transistor manufacturers, which in turn set the pace by which actors across the sector coordinate hardware and software product cycles (Mody 2017). Yet Moore's law and Koomey's law are also deeply imbricated in the cultural and economic expectations of the industries and people ICT touches (which is to say, almost everyone). Steadily improving costs and processing power have established both a reserve army of technological labor and a con-comitant popular mystification of the technology itself (Lison 2020). This growth has also been directly economic; besides Aramco, the five largest companies in the world are Apple, Alphabet, Microsoft, Amazon, and Facebook.

What, then, might it mean that these foundational laws are coming to a close?

The Limits to Growth on a Silicon Wafer

Exponential growth is now no longer a technical surety or a social promise between industry players today—Moore's law is ending, leaving a growing crisis in its wake. Perpetual miniaturization, after all, can't be indefinitely sustained, and in 2010, the doubling of chip densities began to slow as transistor size crept closer to the edge of its material limits. When too few atoms are placed between insulating and conducting spaces within a semiconductor, quantum entanglement begins to complicate the otherwise straightforward electrical engineering of a circuit, creating new and expounding sources of noise in digital signals. Additionally, the socioeconomic apparatus of this trend has come under strain: even though the price per area of silicon has held constant, the overall investment costs in transistor manufacturing have skyrocketed (Mack 2011, 206). As a result, circuit density growth is waning. So, too, is energy efficiency: Koomey's law has slowed to a 2.7-year doubling period.

An end to the industry's impressive growth rates in both technical capacities and financial profits is thus a likely future possibility and a source of considerable present anxiety. Hundreds of millions of dollars in venture capital and untold amounts of industry R&D have been poured into experimental quantum computing research in the hope that a last-minute shift to a fundamentally different set of physics and coding logics might overcome the material limitations of the electrical circuit (Gibney 2019). However, given the extreme thermal environments (and thus energy costs) currently required for these systems, it is not at all clear that they will succeed in replacing the electrons of silicon semiconductors as the medium of computation in the overwhelming majority of contexts.

Absent a revolution in materials, the socially expected pace of technical growth can be maintained—at least for a while—by over-building and offshoring computational work. Indeed, one way to see the rise of cloud computing in recent decades is as a response to the end of Moore's law. Moving more computational storage and processing work to the cloud lets the sector continue to reduce the atoms and electrons within the envelopes of new devices while still offering ever-expanding features. In the process, large shares of the atoms and electrons of computing have been shuffled offstage rather than avoided, sustaining popular beliefs in miniaturization and efficiency even as these expectations enter an era of crisis.

Just as the offshoring of manufacturing at the end of the twentieth century produced a parallel rise in a seemingly immaterial digital/service economy in the Global North, computers themselves are sustained by hidden relations with a distant elsewhere.

But the shift to cloud computing has fundamentally altered the economics of the sector. The electrical costs of digital systems increasingly end up within the ledgers of tech companies rather than the distributed homes and businesses of their customers. This has significant operational impacts; the energy draw of hyperscale server racks makes the ENIAC's generator look quaint. Individual data centers today may commonly use thousands of kilowatts of electricity per hour, every hour and every day, resulting in annual energy costs of roughly $500,000 to $1 million per site (Shi et al. 2018). These expenses rapidly outpace the cost of building the data center itself. Moreover, because of the rise in traffic to and from data centers, network infrastructures have had to scale up their equipment and energy draw. Energy costs alone can now represent as much as 40 to 50 percent of operational expenditures (Lorincz, Capone, and Wu 2019). Flows are now more expensive than stocks.

As such, the ICT sector as a whole has had to think about energy in a new way. Its importance is evident in the organizational charts of virtually all tech companies with hyperscale data center operations. Amazon, Microsoft, Google, Apple, and Facebook have all created senior positions to guide energy procurement and lessen the financial costs of cloud computing. Such factors also heavily weigh on the location choice of new infrastructure: there has been both a large build-out in northern climates to reduce cooling requirements (and therefore the energy costs of operations) and a proliferation of data centers in states where coal power and deregulation have led to cheap energy markets (Cook and Jardim 2019). If, as Microsoft's general manager of energy states, "electricity is really the raw material of a cloud" (Lacey and Kann 2018), then the cloud represents a turn toward a kind of manufacturing logic that has been largely absent from a sector that otherwise depends on a thick web of third-party contractors to do the work of sourcing and assembling physical goods. The work that was offshored has, in part, come back home.

This shift is visible in global energy and climate trends to a growing degree. Data centers presently consume more than two hundred terawatt-hours of electricity a year—roughly 1 percent of total global energy demand. This is mirrored by network operations, which require a roughly equivalent share of additional energy (International Energy Agency 2020) and are growing on pace with Moore's law (Malmodin and Lundén 2018, 24). As such, the ICT sector as a whole is responsible for approximately 2.7 percent of annual global greenhouse gas emissions, on par with the aviation industry or the nation of Germany (Lorincz, Capone, and Wu 2019).

In the context of worsening climate change, this is cause for present concern. However, the stakes of ICT energy use are most acute when examining its future trajectories. Exponential trends, to this end, now work against the industry's public image. Extrapolating from the rise of data center build-out in the 2010s, some scholars estimated that the sector could balloon out to 8 percent (Ferreboeuf 2019, 17) or even up to 51 percent (Andrae and Edler 2015) of global energy use in the next decade if growth rates are maintained, creating parallel disasters in energy access and carbon emissions. Such figures often circulate in news coverage about the "tsunami" of data growth expected in the next five to ten years (Vidal 2017), with the number of Internet-connected devices expected to double between 2019 and 2025 (International Energy Agency 2017).

Industry heads and researchers, however, are not so alarmed— energy efficiency, they hold, will again save the day. Drawing on more recent data, several studies have demonstrated that, despite this considerable growth in data center and network traffic, the flows of emissions and energy associated with these activities have been almost entirely flat for the past decade (Malmodin and Lundén 2018; Masanet et al. 2020). While the reconfiguration of computing power in the initial build-out of the data center industry did create a large spike in emissions and energy draw, a rapid move toward more efficient data center cooling systems and server designs that better manage idle power consumption has prevented the material and economic growth of the industry from producing a commensurate degree of climate impacts and operating expenses (Shehabi et al. 2018). Koomey feels vindicated: his law still holds (albeit, only if you adjust the metric from peak-use efficiency to instead consider "typical use"). And so, the spirit of Moore's law lives on in a new frontier of energy savings, at least for the near future: "even though the fundamental physics is working against us, it appears we'll have a reprieve" (Koomey and Naffziger 2015). Researchers even speak of this efficiency as a "resource" that can be exploited to "absorb the next doubling" of network data (Masanet et al. 2020, 985). Exponential efficiency gains have, again, buttressed computation's exponential growth.

This fact sets ICT apart from other industries; it has to some significant degree decoupled its rate of economic growth from its most obvious forms of environmental impact. As such, it is a rare example of green growth—or at least evidence in support of the possibility of such a thing. In the context of rapidly accelerating climate change, this is a discursively valuable sign: it suggests that climate and capitalism might not be fundamentally at odds and that a turn to a more digital economic base may be the way through the environmental challenges of the coming decades. In some schools of thought, in addition to electrifying as much of the economy as possible to accelerate a transition away from fossil fuels, we may need to Internet of Things (IoT) everything as well, using networks and artificial intelligence (AI) to ensure the most efficient distribution of energy, goods, and capital in the context of a coming resource squeeze. The European Union's (EU) Green Deal therefore names digital technologies as a "critical enabler" of its sustainability goals, for both monitoring and optimization purposes (European Commission 2019, 10). Similarly, the Global e-Sustainability Initiative (an industry consortium working in part-nership with the United Nations Framework Convention on Climate

Change and the World Business Council for Sustainable Development) argues that the efficiency gains of the ICT sector provide a pathway to economic decoupling for global industry at large. On the basis of undisclosed data, it asserts that ICT can reduce global, cross-sectoral greenhouse gas emissions by 20 percent by 2030, thereby fundamentally avoiding "the tradeoff between economic prosperity and environmental protection" (Accenture Strategy 2015, 8). What's more, these future savings are estimated to outweigh the carbon footprint of the sector by tenfold (Accenture Strategy 2015, 10). Koomey's law, in other words, will not only save ICT; it will save the world.

One thus sees the tech sector overrepresented at events where capital gathers to tell stories about itself to itself. Before the Covid-19 pandemic, this included Davos hype about the fourth industrial revolution: a hypothesized transformational turn to IoT, AI, and renewables at the economic and social base of society. More recently, discourse has turned toward the idea of "stakeholder capitalism": a vision for corporations as profitable problem solvers, guided by a renewed sense of social purpose (World Economic Forum 2020). ICT features prominently in the businesses and CEOs rallying behind the name. It was also a vocal part of the We Are Still In contingent of American businesses pledging continued support for the Paris Agreement after the Trump administration's withdrawal, as well as domestic efforts to improve the prospects of carbon taxes and green energy markets. At multiple scales, the sector has pushed itself forward as the banner-holders of green economic growth in an era of multiple intersecting crises.

This future is not uncontested; intraclass struggle at the top of the economy is a growing and underexplored component of contemporary climate politics. Many of the green energy moves made by ICT companies bring them into conflict with the fossil fuel interests that have otherwise enjoyed pride of place as the largest corporations in the world. Climate advocacy, after all, threatens oil and gas profits. Indeed, in many political arenas—such as a 2018 Washington State ballot initiative supporting a carbon tax, a 2016 amicus brief in support of the Clean Power Plan, and a 2021 congressional letter in support of a federal clean energy standard—large ICT companies have lined up with lobbying dollars and political weight on the opposite side of fossil fuel interests. It's enough that some on the climate left have looked to Big Tech as a valued coalitional partner in the larger fight against Big Oil (Buck 2021, 118).

Yet, in other respects, the boundaries between the two are growing murkier. As many note, Microsoft, Google, and Amazon (among many other, smaller players) are increasingly essential partners to the extraction of oil and gas resources. AI analytics and IoT have replaced much of the labor costs of seismic exploration and reservoir modeling, while also increasing the pool and profitability of potential reserves. The future expansion of such tools in the sector is seen as both likely and essential to the further development of "tight" fossil resources, such as those obtained through fracking (International Energy Agency 2017). At the same time as tech companies have become increasingly essential suppliers to fossil energy companies, fossil energy companies have become increasingly essential suppliers to tech. Microsoft, for example, recently invested in afforestation projects by Shell Energy and has a much longer history of renewable energy contracting from Shell and BP. The joint buying and selling of services between these companies has the pattern of business strategy: a smaller renewable energy purchasing commitment on the part of the tech giant often follows a much larger and more lucrative contract to offer AI, cloud computing, or IoT services to the energy giant (Tough 2020). If Big Tech does succeed in bringing down Big Oil, it might do so more through a process of incorporation and synthesis than through straightforward conflict—they may simply become the same industry (Buck 2021, 115). In this way, an energy analytic of ICT will be ever more essential to understanding its contradictory directions.

Yet this focus on efficiency so key to developing and maintaining the sector's identity and business models has obscured the larger picture—it mistakes stocks for flows. While the carbon and energy intensities of data storage and network transmission continue to fall, the total stock of the industry's infrastructure and energy needs is still creeping upward. Additionally, the wider carbon savings of ICT in its applications in other industries are not as certain as industry consortia or the EU Green Deal would suggest: rebound effects and more detailed life cycle analysis efforts all complicate the surety with which we can make such assertions (Sorrell, Gatersleben, and Druckman 2020; Court and Sorrell 2020). "Electric environmentalism," as Jennifer Gabrys (2014, 14) calls it, will thus forever be to some degree a paradoxical thing: the wider material and social relations that green sensors and efficiencies afford are both helpful and themselves harmful. We currently lack robust empirical evidence that the overall gains outweigh the harms or that the sector will soon accelerate in an environmentally positive direction (Freitag et al. 2021).

What's more, recourse to energy efficiency—that dam holding back the flood of proliferating data centers—is another kind of growth that cannot be sustained indefinitely. The race between Koomey's law and booming data center construction has a final horizon: when the idle power required for typical use efficiency creeps close to zero, it will no longer be possible for efficiencies to double— this resource will run out. The industry is estimated to reach this horizon in about a decade's time (Koomey and Naffziger 2015). As a recent meta-analysis of the question concludes, "this fundamentally calls into question the presumed role of efficiency within climate strategy" (Freitag et al. 2021, 36).

Coda: A New Course for Electrons?

Digital operations today are energy operations. Taking this view on the history and future of the industry reveals that it has almost always been in the business of atoms and electrons and that tensions between the two have established expectations and contradictions that are increasingly coming to a head. Computation allows for electrically mediated connections that are, in the mechanics of their operations, ways of communicating across matter and distance through means that are not immaterial but certainly

pose the question of materiality differently. At first, this difference
provided labor- and time-saving efficiencies, informed by management needs and military directions. This orientation was later
internalized and extended in Moore's and Koomey's laws, which let
the ICT industry grow prolifically without a commensurately sized
material footprint. As such, miniaturization and energy efficiency
became guiding logics for the sector and help explain its unprec-
edented capital gains and green reputation. Yet the centrality
of efficiency and exponential growth expectations has also constrained a reckoning with the material limits of these trends as well
as the problem of the overall energy and carbon stocks associated
with the industry. And so, both in triumph and in crisis, the materiality and economics of computing are fundamentally intertwined
with the viability of energy efficiency as a management strategy.
This leaves us at a juncture where the future prospects of ICT (and
perhaps capitalism more broadly) are newly bound to the question
of stocks rather than flows; the atoms that were bracketed out
of the central part of this story of growth are now returning to
the forefront of sectoral interests and anxieties. Meanwhile, the
global data center industry is set to double its computing instances
again in the next three years (Cisco 2018). The problem cannot be
deferred for long.

One way that wealthy tech companies have responded to this
impasse is by integrating energy-associated emissions into their
enterprise accounting structures, nominally claiming the carbon
atoms associated with the production of their electrical supply.
Microsoft, Apple, and Google have for several years been carbon
neutral via the purchase of carbon offsets and renewable energy
certificates—typically in the form of questionable forestry and wind
projects that are more symbol than material action (Pasek 2019).[5]
Yet, as energy has become a C-Suite preoccupation, so, too, has
climate action. Energy managers have been put to work negotiating
direct contracts with renewable energy suppliers, as ICT now makes
up about half of all global corporate green energy procurement,
outpacing all other sectors (BloombergNEF 2020). These actions

are still insufficient to meet the scale of data center demand, but
they are, at least, an attempt to economically reconnect the flows
of electrons and atoms across the carbon cycle.

And these attempts have inspired many more. Microsoft recently
announced that it aims to be not only carbon neutral but carbon
negative—committing to removing carbon emissions associated
with its ongoing and historical environmental impacts going back
to the founding of the company. This has required that managers
invent new accounting protocols and allocate a billion dollars in
investments for nascent carbon removal companies, doing with
private money what public actors have only just begun to discuss
(Microsoft Corporation 2021). Google, on its end, has led in the
creation of a 24/7 carbon-free electricity plan to guide its energy
strategy, going beyond national and international standards and
spurring energy providers to publish new forms of data that help
fill in existing reporting gaps and uncertainties (Google 2020). Such
initiatives push markets, regulatory standards, and grid design
in ways that are genuinely useful in the wider multistakeholder
responses required by fast-approaching climate targets. They also
deepen the ways in which tech companies are imbricated in the
management and ownership of energy companies more broadly.
At best, these developments can be a way of leveraging the huge
capital bases of these corporations to accelerate climate action.
More cynically, it's unclear how far these efforts will go toward
hastening a wider retirement of the fossil fuel industry as a whole
or doing more than just intensifying the size and monopoly power
of ICT's largest players. In either respect, actual degrowth does
not yet appear to be on the figurative table; there is instead every
effort being made to sustain Moore's law in its inglorious afterlife,
attempting to retroactively and yet still insufficiently undo the
material impacts it has caused. And so the contradictions of energy
efficiency remain. All that we can be certain of is that it is stocks—
rather than rates of flow—that will ultimately decide the question.
Efficiency alone can no longer manage the distance between
electrons and atoms.

Notes

1 This idea is briefly mentioned by Hughes (2005, 108).
2 Assuming that 80 soldier crabs are required to run a logic gate, 640,000 crabs would apparently be needed to store the information in a tweet. https://twitter .com/emollick/status/1371932428982493185.
3 For more on the role of conductive media in establishing core terms and theoretical problems in the field of media studies, see Sprenger (2020).
4 For more on the thermocultures of computing, see Starosielski (2021) and chapter 2 of this volume.
5 Facebook and Amazon are following in their footsteps, with net zero targets set for 2030 and 2040, respectively.

References

Accenture Strategy. 2015. *#SMARTer2030: ICT Solutions for 21st Century Challenges.* Brussels: Global e-Sustainability Initiative. https://smarter2030.gesi.org/down loads/Full_report.pdf.

Adamatzky, Andrew, and Theresa Schubert. 2014. "Slime Mold Microfluidic Logical Gates." *Materials Today* 17, no. 2: 86–91. https://doi.org/10.1016/j.mattod.2014 .01.018.

Andrae, Anders S. G., and Tomas Edler. 2015. "On Global Electricity Usage of Communication Technology: Trends to 2030." *Challenges* 6, no. 1: 117–57. https://doi.org/ 10.3390/challe6010117.

Blanchette, Jean-François. 2011. "A Material History of Bits." *Journal of the American Society for Information Science and Technology* 62, no. 6: 1042–57. https://doi.org/ 10.1002/asi.21542.

BloombergNEF. 2020. "Corporate PPA Tracker: March 2020." https://www.bnef.com/ core/insights/22615.

Buck, Holly Jean. 2021. *Ending Fossil Fuels: Why Net Zero Is Not Enough.* New York: Verso.

Bullynck, Maarten. 2019. "Switching the Engineer's Mind-Set to Boolean: Applying Shannon's Algebra to Control Circuits and Digital Computing (1938–1958)." In *Exploring the Early Digital,* edited by Thomas Haigh, 87–99. Cham, Switzerland: Springer. https://doi.org/10.1007/978-3-030-02152-8.

Chun, Wendy Hui Kyong. 2006. *Control and Freedom: Power and Paranoia in the Age of Fiber Optics.* Cambridge, Mass.: MIT Press.

Cisco. 2018. "Cisco Global Cloud Index: Forecast and Methdology, 2016–2021." https://cloud.report/whitepapers/cisco-global-cloud-indexforecast-and-method ology2016%e2%80%932021.

Cook, Gary, and Elizabeth Jardim. 2019. "Clicking Clean Virginia: The Dirty Energy Powering Data Center Alley." Greenpeace. https://www.greenpeace.org/usa/ reports/click-clean-virginia/.

Court, Victor, and Steven Sorrell. 2020. "Digitalisation of Goods: A Systematic Review

of the Determinants and Magnitude of the Impacts on Energy Consumption."
Environmental Research Letters 15, no. 4: 043001. https://doi.org/10.1088/1748
-9326/ab6788.

Ensmenger, Nathan, and Rebecca Slayton. 2017. "Computing and the Environment:
Introducing a Special Issue of Information and Culture." *Information and Culture:
A Journal of History* 52, no. 3: 295–303. https://doi.org/10.1353/lac.2017.0011.

European Commission. 2019. "The European Green Deal." December 11. https://
ec.europa.eu/info/sites/default/files/european-green-deal-communication_en.pdf.

Ferreboeuf, Hughes. 2019. "Lean ICT: Towards Digital Sobriety." The Shift Project.
https://theshiftproject.org/wp-content/uploads/2019/03/Lean-ICT-Report_The
-Shift-Project_2019.pdf.

Fredkin, Edward, and Tommaso Toffoli. 1982. "Conservative Logic." *International Journal of Theoretical Physics* 21, no. 3: 219–53. https://doi.org/10.1007/BF01857727.

Freitag, Charlotte, Mike Berners-Lee, Kelly Widdicks, Bran Knowles, Gordon Blair, and
Adrian Friday. 2021. "The Climate Impact of ICT: A Review of Estimates, Trends and
Regulations." http://arxiv.org/abs/2102.02622.

Gabrys, Jennifer. 2014. "Powering the Digital: From Energy Ecologies to Electronic
Environmentalism." In *Media and the Ecological Crisis,* edited by Richard Maxwell,
Jon Raundalen, and Nina Lager Vestberg, 3–18. New York: Taylor and Francis.

Galison, Peter. 2000. "Einstein's Clocks: The Place of Time." *Critical Inquiry* 26, no. 2:
355–89. http://www.jstor.org/stable/1344127.

Gibney, Elizabeth. 2019. "Quantum Gold Rush: The Private Funding Pouring into
Quantum Start-Ups." *Nature* 574, no. 7776: 22–24. https://doi.org/10.1038/d415
86-019-02935-4.

Google. 2020. "24/7 by 2030: Realizing a Carbon-Free Future." https://www.gstatic
.com/gumdrop/sustainability/247-carbon-free-energy.pdf.

Guizzo, Erico Marui. 2003. "The Essential Message: Claude Shannon and the Making
of Information Theory." MS thesis, Massachusetts Institute of Technology. https://
dspace.mit.edu/handle/1721.1/39429.

Gunji, Yukio-Pegio, Yuta Nishiyama, and Andrew Adamatsky. 2011. "Robust Soldier
Crab Ball Gate." *Complex Systems* 20, no. 2: 93–104. https://doi.org/10.25088/
ComplexSystems.20.2.93.

Hogan, Mél. 2015. "Data Flows and Water Woes: The Utah Data Center." *Big Data and
Society* 2, no. 2: 1–12. https://doi.org/10.1177/2053951715592429.

Hughes, Thomas P. 2005. *Human-Built World: How to Think about Technology and
Culture.* Chicago: University of Chicago Press.

International Energy Agency. 2017. *Digitalisation and Energy.* Paris: IEA. https://www
.iea.org/reports/digitalisation-and-energy.

International Energy Agency. 2020. *Data Centres and Data Transmission Networks.* Paris:
IEA. https://www.iea.org/reports/data-centres-and-data-transmission-networks.

Johnson, Alix. 2019. "Emplacing Data within Imperial Histories: Imagining Iceland as
Data Centers' 'Natural' Home." *Culture Machine* 18 (April). https://culturemachine
.net/vol-18-the-nature-of-data-centers/emplacing-data/.

Kittler, Friedrich A. 1999. *Gramophone, Film, Typewriter.* Translated by Geoffrey
Winthrop-Young and Michael Wutz. Stanford, Calif.: Stanford University Press.

40   Kline, Ronald R. 2019. "Inventing an Analog Past and a Digital Future in Computing."
          In *Exploring the Early Digital,* edited by Thomas Haigh, 19–39. Cham, Switzerland:
          Springer. https://doi.org/10.1007/978-3-030-02152-8.

Koomey, Jonathan G., and Samuel Naffziger. 2015. "Moore's Law Might Be Slowing
          Down, but Not Energy Efficiency." *IEEE Spectrum,* March 31. https://spectrum.ieee
          .org/computing/hardware/moores-law-might-be-slowing-down-but-not-energy
          -efficiency.

Lacey, Stephen, and Shayle Kann. 2018. "Google and Microsoft Are Shaping Ener-
          gy Markets." *The Interchange.* https://www.greentechmedia.com/articles/read/
          google-and-microsoft-are-shaping-energy-markets.

Light, Jennifer S. 1999. "When Computers Were Women." *Technology and Culture* 40,
          no. 3: 455–83. https://doi.org/10.1353/tech.1999.0128.

Lison, Andrew. 2020. "Toward a Theory of 100% Utilization." *Configurations* 28, no. 4:
          491–519. https://doi.org/10.1353/con.2020.0024.

Lorincz, Josip, Antonio Capone, and Jinsong Wu. 2019. "Greener, Energy-Efficient and
          Sustainable Networks: State-of-the-Art and New Trends." *Sensors* 19, no. 22: 4864.
          https://doi.org/10.3390/s19224864.

Mack, Chris A. 2011. "Fifty Years of Moore's Law." *IEEE Transactions on Semiconductor
          Manufacturing* 24, no. 2: 202–7.

Malmodin, Jens, and Dag Lundén. 2018. "The Energy and Carbon Footprint of the
          Global ICT and E&M Sectors 2010–2015." *Sustainability* 10, no. 9: 3027. https://doi
          .org/10.3390/su10093027.

Masanet, Eric, Arman Shehabi, Nuoa Lei, Sarah Smith, and Jonathan Koomey. 2020.
          "Recalibrating Global Data Center Energy-Use Estimates." *Science* 367, no. 6481:
          984–86. https://doi.org/10.1126/science.aba3758.

Mauchly, John W. 1982. "The Use of High Speed Vacuum Tube Devices for Calculat-
          ing." In *The Origins of Digital Computers: Selected Papers,* edited by Brian Randell,
          355–58. Berlin: Springer. https://doi.org/10.1007/978-3-642-61812-3_28.

Maxwell, Richard, and Toby Miller. 2012. *Greening the Media.* New York: Oxford Uni-
          versity Press.

Microsoft Corporation. 2021. *Microsoft Carbon Removal: Lessons from an Early Corpo-
          rate Purchase.* Redmond, Wash.: Microsoft. https://query.prod.cms.rt.microsoft
          .com/cms/api/am/binary/RE4MDlc.

Mills, Mara. 2021. "Hearing Loss and the History of Information Theory." Presented at
          the Assistance, Assistants, and Assistive Media Conference, Leuphana, Germany.

Mody, Cyrus C. M. 2017. *The Long Arm of Moore's Law: Microelectronics and American
          Science.* Cambridge, Mass.: MIT Press.

Naffzinger, Sam, and Jonathan G. Koomey. 2016. "Energy Efficiency of Computing:
          What's Next?" *Electronic Design,* November 28. https://www.electronicdesign.com
          /technologies/microprocessors/article/21802037/energy-efficiency-of-computing
          -whats-next.

Negroponte, Nicholas. 1995. *Being Digital.* New York: Knopf.

Noyce, Robert. 1977. "Microelectronics." *Scientific America,* September.

Parikka, Jussi. 2015. *A Geology of Media.* Minneapolis: University of Minnesota Press.

Park, Lisa Sun-Hee, and David N. Pellow. 2004. "Racial Formation, Environmental

Racism, and the Emergence of Silicon Valley." *Ethnicities* 4, no. 3: 403–24. https://doi.org/10.1177/1468796804045241.

Pasek, Anne. 2019. "Managing Carbon and Data Flows: Fungible Forms of Mediation in the Cloud." *Culture Machine* 18 (April). http://culturemachine.net/vol-18-the-nature-of-data-centers/managing-carbon/.

Pickering, Andrew. 1995. *The Mangle of Practice: Time, Agency, and Science.* Chicago: University of Chicago Press.

Plant, Sadie. 1997. *Zeros + Ones: Digital Women + the New Technoculture.* London: Fourth Estate.

Randall, V. Alexander. 2006. "The Eckert Tapes: Computer Pioneer Says ENIAC Team Couldn't Afford to Fail—and Didn't." *Computerworld,* February 20. https://www.computerworld.com/article/2561559/the-eckert-tapes--computer-pioneer-says-eniac-team-couldn-t-afford-to-fail----and-.html.

Shannon, Claude Elwood. (1937) 1940. "A Symbolic Analysis of Relay and Switching Circuits." MA thesis, Massachusetts Institute of Technology. https://dspace.mit.edu/handle/1721.1/11173.

Shehabi, Arman, Sarah J. Smith, Eric Masanet, and Jonathan Koomey. 2018. "Data Center Growth in the United States: Decoupling the Demand for Services from Electricity Use." *Environmental Research Letters* 13, no. 12: 124030. https://doi.org/10.1088/1748-9326/aaec9c.

Shi, Yuanyuan, Bolun Xu, Di Wang, and Baosen Zhang. 2018. "Using Battery Storage for Peak Shaving and Frequency Regulation: Joint Optimization for Superlinear Gains." *IEEE Transactions on Power Systems* 33, no. 3: 2882–94. https://doi.org/10.1109/TPWRS.2017.2749512.

Sorrell, Steve, Birgitta Gatersleben, and Angela Druckman. 2020. "The Limits of Energy Sufficiency: A Review of the Evidence for Rebound Effects and Negative Spillovers from Behavioural Change." *Energy Research and Social Science* 64 (June): 101439. https://doi.org/10.1016/j.erss.2020.101439.

Sprenger, Florian. 2020. "Temporalities of Instantaneity: Electric Wires and the Media of Immediacy." In *Action at a Distance,* 1–28. Minneapolis: University of Minnesota Press. https://library.oapen.org/handle/20.500.12657/49998.

Starosielski, Nicole. 2015. *The Undersea Network.* Durham, N.C.: Duke University Press.

Starosielski, Nicole. 2021. *Media Hot and Cold.* Durham, N.C.: Duke University Press.

Tough, John. 2020. "Microsoft: The Surprise Energy Wildcatter." *Forbes,* October 7. https://www.forbes.com/sites/johntough/2020/10/07/microsoft-the-surprise-energy-wildcatter/.

Vidal, John. 2017. "'Tsunami of Data' Could Consume One Fifth of Global Electricity by 2025." *The Guardian,* December 11. http://www.theguardian.com/environment/2017/dec/11/tsunami-of-data-could-consume-fifth-global-electricity-by-2025.

War Department. 1946. "Physical Aspects, Operation of ENIAC Are Described." Smithsonian National Museum of American History. https://americanhistory.si.edu/comphist/pr4.pdf.

World Economic Forum. 2020. "Stakeholder Capitalism: What Is Required from Corporate Leadership." IBM Media Center. January 21. https://mediacenter.ibm

42 .com/media/WEF+2020+-+Stakeholder+CapitalismA+What+is+Required+from+-
Corporate+Leadership/0_3ncqkiw2.

This research was supported in part by the Canada Research Chairs program (grant 950-233016). It benefits from conversations with colleagues in the Sustainable Subsea Network.

2

That Which Escapes: Thinking through Heat in Proof-of-Work Systems

Zane Griffin Talley Cooper

The Explosion

It started with an explosion—a violent combustion of excess heat chiseling through the brittle corridors of the circuit like Bresson's (1956) imprisoned resistance fighter, finally bursting out of a small window under a loose capacitor dangling off the motherboard of our cryptocurrency mining machine, which now lay inert, inundated in a transparent vat of nonconductive mineral oil, smoke billowing from its oddly static liquid surface. Freedom at last. That smoke? The smell of a successful escape.

This was not a terribly large explosion, but large enough to raise considerable alarm among the sixteen or so of us gathered in the basement of the Annenberg School for Communication in Philadelphia, awaiting the first trial run of our very own Bitmain Antminer S7 (see Figure 2.1), a rather unsightly aluminum frame containing an assortment of application-specific integrated circuits (ASICs) built and tuned for one purpose and one purpose only—to *generate*[1] cryptocurrency through a process known as proof-of-work. Simply put, proof-of-work is a process by which many computers on a network expend computing cycles (and

[Figure 2.1]. A used Bitmain Antminer S7 with its dedicated power converter, purchased on eBay for the 2019 exhibit *Alchemical Infrastructures: Making Blockchain in Iceland*. Photograph by the author.

energy) to produce bits of hashed data in the service of validating a message. Grounded firmly in the material limitations of information processing and transmission, the concept was originally implemented in the 1990s as a sort of algorithmic "metered postage" to deter mass spam emails (Brunton 2019, 101–2) but has since found new life and new scales in blockchain technology. Using the explosion as an entry point, this chapter explores the materiality of the work in proof-of-work systems through a historical, sociopolitical, and energetic analysis of the heat managed in their antecedent infrastructure and produced in their wake.

By interrogating the *work* in proof-of-work, and situating this work in the broader context of the infrastructural *heat-work* of computing, this chapter attempts to excavate a media archaeology of computational heat to build a more robust vocabulary for how to think and talk about that which escapes and that which is lost through the cracks of digital media infrastructures. Because of their single-purpose designs, proof-of-work systems like Bitcoin can be used as heuristics through which to better understand the material and ideological fundamentals of how data and energy come together on the ground. In part, this requires correcting the narrative of Bitcoin and proof-of-work as exceptional circumstances and the framing of proof-of-work as some sort of obscene outlier in an otherwise efficient and well-functioning computing landscape. Rather, proof-of-work systems have been and continue to be deeply embedded in global computing infrastructure, from manufacturing to data center design. Today, bitcoins are principally generated with proprietary machines called ASICs, which contain specialized microchips designed for single-purpose computing. Although ASICs have been around since the 1970s, Bitcoin almost single-handedly rejuvenated the long-stagnant ASIC market (Taylor 2017), moving the industry rapidly from sectors like calculators and video game consoles into the realm of high-performance computing. Additionally, the stripped-down, modular, high-density data center designs Bitcoin helped model have already been translated to other services like artificial intelligence (AI) and machine learning (Taylor et al. 2020). Many companies that got their start designing and manufacturing ASICs for proof-of-work systems have also begun designing custom AI chips as well, as part of a growing trend to "specialize" the data center (see Khazraee et al. 2017; Magaki et al. 2016).

All this goes to say that, at the infrastructural level, proof-of-work is very similar to, if not functionally indistinguishable from, other practices of high-performance computing. The only thing altogether exceptional about proof-of-work is its ideological inversion of how data processing is interpreted and valued. Rather than under-standing information as a force of negative entropy of no material context (as in Shannon's information theory), proof-of-work systems see information as an outcome of entropy, or expended, irreversible energy use. Kirkwood (2021, 363) notably observes this inversion as well but argues that, because of its valuation of wasted energy, proof-of-work destroys meaning through "computational squander." I argue the opposite. The waste is the point, the meaning in all of this. In proof-of-work systems, expended energy is given meaning and value, thereby pointing directly to a panacea of energetic relations. Because of this ideological inversion, proof-of-work can stand in as a singular expression of digital data's broader industrial energetic relationships and help us understand how they could possibly be different.

Our ASIC was a critical component of an expansive art exhibit exploring the making (or generating) of cryptocurrency in Iceland (Cooper et al. 2019) and actively generated cryptocurrency for the nine-month duration of the exhibit while we recorded its cumulative energy use and revenue. However, on this muggy August morning, a month out from the exhibit's opening, the anxiety was palpable as we prepared to officially switch on the machine for the first time. A common refrain in the cryptocurrency space is that, to generate coins, all you really need is electricity and an internet connection. In practice, however, it becomes far more complicated and depends heavily on geography and available infrastructure.

Cryptocurrency generation is a hot and loud affair. Although our machine had fans on both ends of its rectangular body, if left running unattended, its internal temperature could still climb to well over two hundred degrees Fahrenheit. Additionally, when actively *working,* the machine sounded like an industrial vacuum cleaner, often exceeding ninety decibels. Both the heat and noise were unacceptable for a public exhibit, so, taking a cue from proof-of-work practices in warmer regions like southern China and Texas, we opted to liquid-cool our machine by drowning it in a solution of petroleum-based mineral oil, which can move in, through, and out of the machine without affecting its functionality. This solution mitigated the excess heat and noise and allowed us to monitor the ambient temperature of the tank in which the machine sat (see Figure 2.2). All of this effort and intense preparation led to that fateful day in August, when we finally, at last, threw the switch and started *proving our work,* which we hoped and expected would generate some cryptocurrency. In the end, it did, but not without

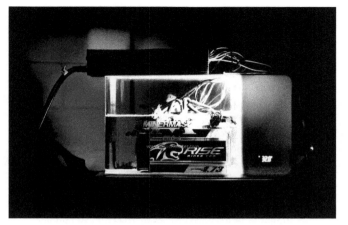

[Figure 2.2]. Our Bitmain Antminer S7, kept relatively quiet and cool in a custom liquid-cooling tank, drowned in petroleum-based mineral oil. Photograph by Kyle Cassidy.

an exceptional amount of ongoing maintenance and wasted energy.

Now to the explosion. Less a boom than a sizzle, the spark ignited immediately after the machine switched on, sending smoke billowing through the gelatinous oil. Upon seeing the gathering smoke, we quickly unplugged the machine and wheeled the entire apparatus outside, where we inspected it and found the culprit: a loose, now scorched, capacitor. Because this capacitor only affected one (of three) of the motherboards, we made the decision simply to unplug that board and continue running our machine with only two-thirds of its computing capacity. The exhibit lived; the show went on. However, although we did not experience another explosion in the next nine months, the container consistenly leaked oil, both into and out of itself, requiring constant, almost surgical maintenance with oil syringes and ever so much gauze.

I begin with this personal tale of combustion and maintenance because it calls attention to that which exists on the periphery of computational systems: that which escapes, that which cannot and will not be contained, and that which is lost and unaccounted for. During the course of the exhibit, our little Bitmain Antminer S7 consumed a total of 583.5 kilowatt-hours of electricity, a little less than an average refrigerator would consume in the same amount of time. However, this figure, if taken at face value, obscures the tremendous amount of preparation and maintenance work, the international collaboration, and the excess heat consistently pushed through the viscous oil. There is more beneath and beyond that simple calculated bridge between computation and energy use, between the work and its proof. What falls off in this crossing? What fell off before? What will fall after? A heat-centered energetic analysis can bring us closer to these answers.

If media studies is, as we have discussed, the study of middles (see the introduction to this volume), then how can we access that which is exhausted, lost, and unaccounted for in the perilous journey through these middles? As media travel, they shed, and that shedding blankets other grounds and other media. We hear this shedding with every crackle and interruption of a cell signal, see it every time a video buffers, and feel it when our laptops overheat. As such, the history of electronic communication is also a history of insulation and containment against this shedding (Starosielski 2015; Tully 2009), a perpetual struggle, an often vicious, violent dance between infrastructures of signal and noise, order and chaos (Larkin 2008; Serres 1982). Practices of insulation and containment produce insides and outsides, delineate the wanted and unwanted, which also makes the history of electronic communication a history of waste—of defining it, controlling it, and forgetting it. A central question for discard studies asks, "what must be discarded for this or that system to be created and to carry on?" (Liboiron and Lepawsky 2022, 3). In tracking heat on its journey out of the circuit, this chapter attempts to chart a course across related concepts that all come to matter in the politics of wasting in proof-of-work, and computing infrastructures more broadly: *externality, uncertainty,* and *waste.* These terms are at times used

interchangeably because they are all common travelers through
the conceptual history of thermodynamics on which I argue proof-
of-work ideological formations are built. Moreover, I use the idea
of *escape* to assign a sort of fervent agency to heat, to consider it
not as immediately external, uncertain, or wasteful but rather as an
agential force, altogether essential to the system. Clark and Yusoff
(2014) argue that the history of fire and combustion can be seen
as a move from externalization to internalization and insulation,
in which regimes of heat and combustion are increasingly brought
under greater and more expansive control. They are bounded,
these histories of information and combustion—twin strands of
DNA, linked through shared infrastructures and exchanges. One
does not move without the other. The work needs heat to prove
itself, and that heat will escape, one way or another, via exhaust or
explosion. Let us follow it.

The Escape

As Harney and Moten (2013) explain, "logistics could not contain
what it had relegated to the hold. It cannot." And neither can computers. Digital computing is a logistical practice—one of moving
light and electrons from one place to another, across the microscopic silicon space of a circuit, within the mechanical magnetic
enclosure of the hard drive, and through thousands of kilometers
of spagettified glass draped across the seafloor. As with the science
of logistics more broadly, digital computing, with its seemingly
infinite nesting of black boxes, attempts to manufacture movement
without friction, adaptation without question, and translation without pause (Harney and Moten 2013). Proof-of-work systems, like
Bitcoin, are a bit different. Contrary to the attempted disappearing
acts of general-purpose cloud computing infrastructures over the
last decade, the tactility of Bitcoin generation and proximity to its
heat and metal remain pivotal indexes of its value and functionality. As such, proof-of-work systems are case studies for excavating
and interrogating long-standing assumptions about the relationship between data and energy and what these assumptions

both conceal and reveal about the infrastructural futures of computing.

At all points in the computing process—at the edge of every black box, at the rubbery membrane of every fiber-optic cable—the system struggles and fails to contain the terrible weight of the energy forced through its often precariously grafted forms (Hu 2015; Mattern 2021). The history of digital technology, Starosielski (2021, 196) reminds us, can in part be written as the "coldward course of media"—the ceaseless projection of "thermopower" in the service of constructing and maintaining thermal stability and homogeneity across media infrastructures. Yet, despite this teleological freezing, heat remains ever present in this narrative, a key *index* of the computing going on, wherever it happens to be going. Through the frictions, complications, and at times violence it produces, heat helps us feel and understand the work of computing at a visceral, even biological level. One walk through a data center will convince any *body* that data centers, above even their primary roles as centerers of data, moreso function as "climate bunkers" that work to securitize temperatures in such a way as to make data centers "as impervious to atmospheric carbon as enterprising hackers" (Moro 2021, 3). Furthermore, Brunton (2015) asserts that the work of computation in general, from vacuum tubes to microchips, has always been the work of managing heat, as computation could not function at all without the complex infrastructures built to control its thermal emissions. But this is always a losing game. The bit cannot switch from 0 to 1 and back again without letting something go. Because of this perpetual struggle and assured failure of containment, heat enters and exits the system as a radical element, guarding computational thresholds. It acts as a shapeless transient between what Edwards (1996) calls the "closed world" of computers and the "green world" of people, trees, cats, and, well, everything else. It tacks between the two, a crucial indicator of computing's limitations, its materiality, and its inescapable thermodynamic foundations. This is the locus of Velkova's (2021) thermopolitics—heat as the site where ideological processes

of dematerialization and connection become materialized and
disconnected.

Heat is often considered an unwanted outcome of computing,
something emitted in the wake of productive action. But the
production of heat is defined, anticipated, and managed well
before any computing actually occurs, and a complex assemblage
of actors is responsible for its management. As such, in thinking
through heat, we have "response-abilities," as Haraway (2016, 34)
puts it, to think through and with these relations, sitting with the
"creative uncertainty" heat stirs up and following it through its suc-
cessive computational, energetic, and planetary lives. Boyer (2018)
situates infrastructure as a reservoir of potential energy, a specific
structuring of energetic possibilities in a given system. Infrastructure frames a set of potential futures, while rendering others less
or im-possible. In the case of computational heat, a computer's
design anticipates and sets in place an entire sequence of material
relationships to manage and mitigate the production of heat well
before the device ever reaches a user's hand. As such, while the
production of heat is most definitely an outcome of computing,
the work of its mitigation precedes the act of computation, the
directions of its frictions and flows painstakingly preplanned but
never totally controlled. These are the political-economic structures
of what Starosielski (2021, 7) calls "thermopower," by which the mediation of temperature enacts power across biological, geological,
and energetic systems. Containing and managing heat is a political
process at the center of computing practice.

Although proof-of-work, at the material level, is not terribly
different from other kinds of high-performance computing (such as
graphics rendering or machine learning), the interpretation of systems of value through proof-of-work requires a radically visible, intimately material relationship between information and energy—a
relationship that has always been dirty, messy, heavy, and, above
all things, extremely hot. While the fundamental material work
of all digital computing depends entirely on proper handling of
heat, proof-of-work systems conceptually foreground the complex

relationship between data, energy, work, and heat, bringing them into much more nakedly explicit view than ever before.

This visibility is due in part to the character of proof-of-work systems as primarily single-purpose data practices, meaning that all consumed energy is directed to only one task. In the case of Bitcoin, this task is the repeated running of the SHA-256 algorithm, which works to solve randomized equations in the service of validating "blocks" of transactions on the Bitcoin blockchain. The computer (or group of computers) responsible for finally solving the equation and validating a given block is awarded newly generated coins. Bitcoin's algorithm is rather simple, almost elegantly so, but because it runs over and over again, millions of times a second, it quickly becomes a processor-intensive practice that consumes a tremendous amount of energy. Additionally, because scarcity is hard-coded into the Bitcoin network (there will only ever be twenty-one million bitcoins), as more bitcoins enter circulation, the computing power and energy required to validate blocks increases exponentially and almost asymptotically. As such, the network has scaled dramatically from a computing practice performed largely on laptops to a massive, global industrial enterprise comprising hundreds, perhaps thousands, of data centers all over the world.

As infrastructures for proof-of-work systems have scaled, so, too, has the naked visibility of the irreconciliable problems of energy and heat at the center of the proof-of-work model. At the time of this writing, estimates place the Bitcoin network's energy consumption at around 139.06 terawatt-hours per year, an amount comparable to the nation of Ukraine (De Vries 2021). Though Bitcoin's energy problem has become increasingly salient in both academic and popular discourse (see Lally et al. 2019; McKenzie 2021; Mora et al. 2018), the idea of proof-of-work is rarely substantively critiqued beyond its general lambasting as "useless" and calls for the practice to be banned altogether (Bateman 2021). Although I do not disagree that proof-of-work—especially at the current industrial scale of proof-of-work blockchains like Bitcoin— is a dangerously wasteful computing practice, I argue that rather than see it as an exception, we consider more how it points to broader concerns about computing's relationship to energy. Perhaps we should ban proof-of-work, but in doing so, we must understand that calling to ban it does not necessarily address the root of the rot. It merely asserts a value proposition, making a cut that separates good data from bad data. This cut inevitably blames proof-of-work for the broader toxicity of data's energetic relationships, which proof-of-work tends to bring into relief. In other words, if Bitcoin disappeared tomorrow, much of the material capital currently dedicated to proof-of-work would have little problem shifting to other services that may not be quite proof-of-work in name or outcome but would closely resemble it in practice. Proof-of-work is a profoundly visible symptom of a wider and much more complex pathology of digital energetics.

Cryptocurrency generation is often portrayed as a fringe activity, conducted in relative opacity, in abandoned warehouses on the outskirts of rotting industrial parks (see Young 2019), and shunned by the data center industry writ large as unrepresentative of their core business (Masanet et al. 2020; Shehabi et al. 2016). In reality, proof-of-work cryptocurrency generation regularly occurs in "traditional" data center spaces alongside other high-density computing services, such as machine learning and graphics rendering. Bitcoin has only grown so rapidly because it has been able to situate itself in these spaces as an adaptable kind of high-performance computing practice. Bitcoin ASICs first came on the market in 2013, and by 2014, colocation data centers began hosting them in racks right alongside more traditional server configurations (Miller 2014). Even as Bitcoin-specific data centers have proliferated, proof-of-work computing remains firmly embedded in what some would view the more "traditional" data center industry (Masanet et al. 2020).

This infrastructural game of hide-and-seek is especially apparent in Iceland, often framed as a "natural home" for data centers because of the stability of its cold climate (Johnson 2019b). Iceland's state business development ministry even fully embraces this climatic mantra, calling Iceland "the coolest place for data centers" (Invest in Iceland, n.d.). This represents part of a wider thermopolitical strategy (Velkova 2021) stretching across the greater Arctic, using cool climates to frame the region as future oriented and the ideal location for data-driven infrastructure. Iceland's data center industry has been rapidly expanding since 2010, yet, what largely goes unsaid is that most of this growth has come from proof-of-work infrastructure. In 2018, no less than 90 percent of all the energy used for data centers in the country was dedicated to proof-of-work cryptocurrency generation (KPMG 2018), and until late 2019, up to 80 percent of all Icelandic data center clients were cryptocurrency miners. In short, proof-of-work built Iceland's now robust data center industry, even if, since 2020, many of the largest companies have explicitly moved away from cryptocurrency mining as a core business.

Distinct from cryptocurrency generation in other regions like the United States and (formerly) China, a vast majority of the proof-of-work infrastructure in Iceland is housed on the grounds of what outwardly appear as traditional colocation facilities, and primarily at a single site—atNorth's ICE02 data center campus outside of Keflavik, which currently has ten separate warehouses. Although the ICE02 campus mostly hosts cryptocurrency infrastructure—including Genesis Mining, the world's largest cloud mining[2] service (Real Vision 2021)—cryptocurrency is not featured as one of atNorth's primary services but rather one of multiple hosting solutions, including high-performance computing and AI. Additionally, Verne Global's Keflavik data center, located on the site of a former U.S. military base (Johnson 2019a), has hosted cryptocurrency infrastructure since at least 2014 (Richmond 2018), but has recently committed to phasing out its proof-of-work business entirely. It is impossible to know exactly how many cryptocurrency companies exist in Iceland, but the regional topography of the industry illustrates how proof-of-work has scaled both within and without what some consider more traditional data center spaces.

Iceland is a productive geography from which to think about proof-of-work because, though cryptocurrency continues to dominate

Iceland's data center industry, most companies have largely
scrubbed cryptocurrency "mining" from their home pages, favoring
instead language like "blockchain services" or even just simply
"high-performance computing." The Borealis Data Center outside
of Blönduós in North Iceland hosts a number of high-performance
computing services, vaguely identified "blockchain solutions,"
and has a partnership with Kaiser Global for the development of
high-tech science research coalitions. However, when I visited in
2019, the entire data center campus (all six houses) were filled with
thousands of Bitmain Antminer S9s, all actively generating Bitcoin
with an energy capacity of thirty-two megawatts per hour, which,
for North Iceland, is a tremendous amount. For reference, the
entire town of Blönduós uses about 1.5 megawatts per hour. The
shifting categories of these data center services illustrates
the rhetorical fungibility of proof-of-work, the degree to which
the term can be mapped onto and off of different topologies of
social value. This fungibility has little relation to the actual assemblage of ASICs on the ground and as such draws attention to the
strategic opacities forming around proof-of-work infrastructures
that attempt to disguise their alleged uselessness under the veil
of other, less affectively charged, more "acceptable" computing
practices like AI, machine learning, and high-performance
computing.

This is largely a rhetorical and conceptual pivot, rather than a
material one. Over the last few years, the idea of proof-of-work
has grown associated with profound waste and ecological harm,
becoming significantly affectively charged in both popular and academic discourse. Behind the collective recoiling at proof-of-work
lies a broader conceptual history of digital energetics that must be
further excavated. Because proof-of-work makes more profoundly
visible the material and energetic dependencies of digital computing, it forces us to confront, in often uncomfortable ways, digital
information's opaque theoretical and material entanglements with
the history of thermodynamics—a dirty, coal-stained history that,
through decades of mathematical abstraction beginning in the

late nineteenth century, became mostly delinked from modern information science.

Digital computing cannot function without the spinning up of heat, yet the production and disposal of heat are largely absent from information theory, even though the concept of entropy (adapted from the second law of thermodynamics) remains central to how information scientists think about information and its relationship to signal and noise (Serres 1982; Shannon and Weaver 1949). Throughout the 1940s and 1950s, notably at the Macy Conferences on Cybernetics, explicit moves were made to shift ideas about information away from its situatedness within the thermodynamics of heat and toward more abstract, fungible, contextless, and *meaningless* frames. Claude Shannon, for one, heavily influenced by Gibbs's theories of statistical mechanics (Shannon and Weaver 1949), defined information as first and foremost a "probability function with no dimensions, no materiality, and no necessary connection with meaning" (Hayles 1999). In this way, information became a proxy for control and order in a given system, for which the system's materiality and production of heat were considered as waste, externalized, and rendered incidental (Hayles 1999; Kline 2015). This act of wasting is a "technique of power" (Liboiron and Lepawsky 2022, 3) that has increasingly migrated the visibility of computing's heat problems away from end users, offloading them into mammoth data centers, tucked away, out of sight. Here computer and architectural engineers work in relative opacity to direct heat through and out of the viscous darkness of vast infrastructural black boxes.

What would it look like to recenter problems of energy consumption, heat, and loss back into information theory? Scholars of technology and infrastructure have been building this critique for some time. Nathan Ensmenger (2018, S14) situates computing, and the internet in particular, after Thomas P. Hughes, as a "large technological system," tethered to infrastructures of energy, politics, and social life. Similarly, Sy Taffel (2021, 13) argues that data must be considered as embedded deeply in the "metabolic rift" of contemporary carbon capitalism. Furthermore, Josh Lepawsky (2018) vastly expands the geographies and political economies of electronic waste systems by situating electronic waste within its larger industrial, sociopolitical, and geological contexts. "The problem of knowing waste," he surmises, "is partly a problem of what to count and where" (96). Translating these ideas to the realms of information theory, and its conceptual ancestor, thermodynamics, designations of waste in digital systems are deeply related to considerations of order versus chaos or certainty versus uncertainty. These designations are not simply material moves, but ideological and material ones as well. Through these moves, the physical production of heat, and its overwhelming tendency to escape the clutches of closed systems, becomes abstracted into *entropy*—at once a chaotic element, a waste product to be discarded, and an uncertainty to be exhausted.

The (Un)certainty

In May 2019, in a ballroom of the global headquarters of financial services giant Fidelity Investments, Fidelity's Center for Applied Technology convened the #MiningSummit. A veritable who's who of the crypto world gathered for a wide-ranging discussion on the institutions and infrastructures of the cryptocurrency *mining* industry. In the mid-afternoon, during a panel on the "future of mining," moderator Meltem Demirors, former oil and gas lobbyist turned crypto expert, launched into a discussion of the increasingly controversial topic of Bitcoin's monstrous energy use and what, if anything, should be done about it. In response, Dovey Wan, founding partner of a crypto asset investment holding company, posited that Bitcoin is quite literally saving the universe through thermodynamic consensus. She explained,

> "I have a very fundamental theory on why Bitcoin is actually efficient from a thermodynamics perspective. We know, our entire human being, we actually try to fight entropy growth, right? And then so, like, when entropy

grows to the max, and then we die . . . and then . . . the whole universe, and from a cosmos perspective, entropy has to grow . . ." Demirors interjected, "Well, you need chaos to have order, and order to have chaos. Two sides of the same coin." Wan replied, "So that's like, what the Bitcoin network has been doing is . . . actually forming the consensus, and bringing the order, and then to fight the internal entropy growth, right? And then the thing is that at the macro level, our cosmos is actually expanding. And then . . . the general universe, entropy is always positive. And that's why in order to fight that single system's entropy growth, you have to dump that entropy on someone else, so that's why there's no decent cryptography secure consensus that can form without any energy consumption. So from a thermodynamic perspective, it makes sense. It's scientific!" (Soluna 2019, 9:55–11:09)

Proof-of-work systems depend on narratives of certainty to reify their security. These narratives assert that the security of the Bitcoin network's consensus mechanisms draws directly from the thermodynamic laws of the cosmos itself and relies on these laws as immutable certainties. As such, proof-of-work systems foreground computing's direct thermodynamic relations in unique ways that explicitly call back to the rise of the energy concept in the late nineteenth century—a concept that reframed the idea of doing work as something exhaustable, directional, and irreversible (Prigogine and Stengers 1984). The science of thermodynamics redefined what work meant, and, as Daggett (2019) illustrates, this redefinition of work as a scarce, exhaustible, irrecoverable assest became a necessary tool for the expansion of empire and capital. Energy and work, which Newtonian dynamics had defined as renewable and reversible, thermodynamics rendered as discretely quantifiable, exhaustible, and irreversible. Suddenly energy and work were scarce and only moved in one direction—toward progress.

The certainty of irreversible energy is the ideological heart of proof-of-work. One central problem with this framework is that thermodynamics is not, and never has been, a science of certainty. Rather, it is quite literally a science of uncertainty, its laws often as culturally and conceptually elastic as the phenomena they describe. In her discussion, Wan centers the concept of entropy and situates Bitcoin as a sort of bulwark against inevitable entropy growth because it "brings the order," manufacturing consensus from computational and energetic chaos. But entropy, both as a concept and as a physical process, is far from inevitable, especially in systems as open and differentially entangled with other systems as our global computing infrastructures. The laws of energy are not so much natural laws as they are "semantic entities" and "responses to natural forces" (Daggett 2019, 46), with an embedded religious politics heavily influenced by nineteenth-century ideals of industrial progress and a Scottish Presbyterian desire to align that industrial progress with God's will (Daggett 2019; Smith 1998). This is especially true of entropy, which is, at best, an *uncertain* concept, elastic to a fault. It has meant and continues to mean many things, its definition(s) largely dependent on context. To understand proof-of-work and its claim that its security and certainty are rooted in the physical laws of thermodynamics, we must first understand how the concept of entropy has traveled and how this travel has affected the closely related ideas of energy and work. All these ideas came of age together in the same nineteenth-century household, and proof-of-*work* is a direct conceptual outcome of these ideas.

Since its inauguration in the mid-nineteenth century, the concept of entropy has migrated and mutated across a multitude of disciplines, including economics, sociology, and information science. But it all began with the experience of loss, of escaping and irrecoverable heat. Clausius first coined the concept of entropy in 1865 as a way to quantify heat loss in coal engines and to classify different hierarchies of "useful" energy in systems that tend, in all instances, toward chaotic, uncertain futures (Daggett 2019, 44–45). In this instance, entropy's first instance, the relation was deeply material and deeply felt as a physical transformation. Heat radiated out from the engine and was lost, never to be used again. Where did this heat go? Why did it go? How do we keep and contain it so that it can remain useful? At its core, the concept of entropy is a question asked to an uncertain future, a probabilistic hedge that guesses at possible outcomes and makes distinctions between what is and is not useful to a given system. Though it seems naturalized today, Daggett illustrates how the concept of entropy, and the idea of irreversible, uncertain loss, was an earth-shattering proposition in the mid-1800s. Not only was energy not conservable and reversible, as Newtonian dynamics had assumed, but entropy seemed to fix the universe in one immovable, irreversible direction—that of maximum entropy, total thermal equilibrium, or the heat-death of the entire cosmos. The heat-death hypothesis may have been the most spatiotemporally expansive application of the entropy theory, but it was part of a growing trend in the late nineteenth century to make use of thermodynamic theories across diverse areas of knowledge.

Entropy entered the scene as a way to conceptualize and deal with industrial energy loss and, in the process, remade general ideas of space and time by spreading like a contagion across knowledge regimes as a means to deal with probabilistic uncertainty. However, in becoming a radical new paradigm of scientific thought (Kuhn 1996), the uncertain science of thermodynamics was wrapped in a veil of social and political certainty that concretized across epistemic contexts, allowing the formerly material concept of entropy (a measurement of energy loss in heat engines) to inform highly variable notions of energy and work in numerous disciplines. This began with Ludwig Boltzmann, James Clerk Maxwell, and Josiah Willard Gibbs's abstraction of energy dissipation into a mathematics of statistical probability in the 1870s and 1880s.

This new mathematics of statistical mechanics moved entropy away from immediate notions of material loss and toward more abstract probabilities of order and chaos. In these new mathematical formulations, entropy no longer had to remain constrained to the heat engine but could be applied to any theoretically closed system that had engine-like qualities. This proved convenient as, like the computer metaphor today, engines were the dominant explanatory metaphor for societal processes in the nineteenth-century industrial world. Most physical, social, and biological systems could be situated in the domain of the engine metaphor. Everything from nations to corporations to bodies could function-ally be considered engines and as such could be brought under scientific control through the principles of thermodynamics. This helped create new ideas of work and its relationship to the newly scarce and discretely quantifiable concept of energy. In this way, work became a directional process measured (in bodies and machines alike) in joules or calories expended and exhausted.

This nascent energy–work paradigm profoundly shaped industrial designs and working conditions in the early twentieth century, eventually finding its way into Henry Ford's assembly line and Taylor's theories of scientific management. Most of these social and economic applications of thermodynamics were wildly imprecise and had little to do with the science of heat, but the certainty in their efficacy and efficiency was encouraged because they intro-duced new and easier ways to extract value for capital and empire (Daggett 2019). This process of extraction paradoxically embedded a sort of epistemological, ideological, and sociological certainty of industrial progress within a science built on foundations of uncertainty, inefficiency, and loss. By the late 1800s, the science of thermodynamics and the idea of entropy (as well as its certainty as an all-encompassing physical, sociological, and economic concept) wielded such a tremendous amount of conceptual power that anyone who so much as questioned the veracity of some of the more expansive claims of thermodynamics (such as Marx and Engels's critiques of the heat-death hypothesis) was discounted as backward thinking (Foster and Burkett 2016).

However, even given the dominance of the energy concept, and the statistical applications of entropy across economics and labor management, the seemingly limitless semantic elasticity of entropy met with resistance well into the 1940s. In 1949, during the Macy

Conferences (where, from 1946 to 1953, cybernetics and information theory were formalized into mainstream scientific paradigms), the role of entropy in information theory was far from settled. The previous year, Claude Shannon had published his landmark paper "A Mathematical Theory of Communication" in the *Bell Systems Technical Journal,* reframing entropy as a communicative concept relating to the probability of noise in the transmission of information. That same year, Norbert Wiener (1948), in his vastly influential book *Cybernetics; or, Control and Communication in the Animal and the Machine,* compared the relationship between signal and noise in information systems to the relationship between order and disorder in Gibbs's statistical mechanics, positing information as an index of systemic order and therefore an agent of what he termed *negative entropy* or *negentropy.* At this first conference gathering since the publication of these two important works, the role of entropy in information theory was a hotly debated topic. In a presentation on the measuring of semantic information, philosopher Yehoshua Bar-Hillel of Hebrew University offered this critique:

> Some of our best thinkers have expressed the view that this analogy is much more than just any analogy, and statements identifying thermodynamics and communicational information theory, requiring a revision of the second principle of thermodynamics, and even statements identifying thermodynamics with logic have been made recently. I believe that these declarations were more than an attempt to explode old-fashioned ways of thinking and to force people to go deeper into the foundations of thermodynamics than they did so far. But, perhaps for the first time in my life, I find myself on the side of the scientific conservatives. I find it utterly unacceptable that the concept of physical entropy, hence an empirical concept, should be identified with the concept of the amount of semantic information, which is a logical concept. (Macy Conference 2016, 705)

I include Bar-Hillel's critique to illustrate how, even though the idea of information as negative entropy eventually became a cornerstone of early cybernetics, the proximity of this claim to the physical phenomena it references was intensely debated and took time to percolate into mainstream scientific thought. This is in part because the migration of entropy into the realm of semantic logic obscured and compartmentalized the firmly material aspects of what Shannon came eventually to call a *bit* (see chapter 1). The transmission of information, especially at the time, through wires and vacuum tubes, was starkly visible as a hot and energy-intensive practice, yet identifying information as *negative entropy* allowed much of the theory behind this practice to be productively abstracted away from its energetic infrastructures (Hayles 1999; Kline 2015). The semantic rendering of information and entropy has since created profound epistemological tensions between the material engineering of information infrastructures and the more astract, contextless theories of information as *negentropy*. Since the 1940s, abstract ideas about relationships between information, energy, and entropy have expanded into collections of cosmological principles and become embedded in nearly every form of contemporary living, from the containerized global logistics industry (Klose 2015) to the proliferation of single-body principles dominating the designs of digital devices. These systems excel at offsetting and externalizing their exhaustive inefficiencies and at maintaining illusions of frictionlessness, even though the logics undergirding their operations remain inextricably tied to assumptions about work and energy that emerged out of the scientific investigations of coal-fired heat engines in the nineteenth century.

Proof-of-work systems ideologically trouble the precarious epistemological boundaries between information theory and engineering and as such can teach us how to better see data infrastructures through the lens of that which escapes them, that which they could not, cannot, contain. While the actual computing going on in proof-of-work is materially not that distinct from any other, where proof-of-work diverges is how this computing is interpreted and valued.

Unlike with other computing practices, the fundamental logic underpinning proof-of-work maps an explicit value proposition between energy consumption and the resultant data, relying on the theoretical irreversibility of energy consumption to enshrine the alleged immutability of the blockchain. In other words, the block-chained data produced through proof-of-work are quite literally a record of consumption, exhaust, and irretrievable loss—an articulation of entropy. Again, all computing produces heat, exhaust, and entropy, but proof-of-work explicitly acknowledges these material constraints and assigns them value. This is an ideological claim that fundamentally conflicts with popular understandings of what information is and how it moves.

The idea of information as negative entropy presupposes that information naturally decreases entropy growth and, as such, increases efficiency in a given system. The more information, the less entropy! However, proof-of-work inverts this concept, framing blockchained information as a direct outcome of entropic loss, foregrounding the absolute necessity of this loss in the computing process. In her comments at the Fidelity #MiningSummit, Wan identifies this loss and cites its necessary externalization, the need to "dump the entropy onto someone else." In a way, proof-of-work systems try to hold together two cognitively dissonant forces. At once, they attempt to reclaim entropy's dynamic material energetics, while at the same time retaining its semantic qualities through familiar processes of externalization—as Wan would say, dumping the entropy onto someone else.

Many advocates of proof-of-work see increasing energy use and irreversible exhaust as points of pride, as these processes theoretically secure the network. The loss is the point. The exhaust is the *proof* of the *work.* This was already deeply understood by Bitcoin's early adopters:

> We are all ceremonially burning computer cycles as an investment of resources in a "trust pool." The irreversibility of the process—the face that we are burning our com-

putational wheat crop just to crank out unusually numeri-
cally small hashes—is definitely perverse, and deliberately
so. The entirely stupid amount of resources wasted minting bitcoins makes it nigh-impossible that anyone would
choose to be EVEN STUPIDER as to waste the amount of
resources necessary to outcompute you. (Gridecon 2010)

This idea of deliberate thermodynamic perversity has concretized
into an assemblage of loosely gathered and vaguely defined
ideologies about proof-of-work as a purely scientific, almost *natural*
process. Michael Saylor, CEO of enterprise cloud security company
MicroStrategy, trained engineer, and Bitcoin evangelist, consistently professes Bitcoin's purity by claiming that Bitcoin is a "monetary
energy network" forever secured by the laws of thermodynamics.
"Once you understand . . . Bitcoin is a monetary energy network,
then you start to appreciate the fact that it either does or does
not respect the laws of thermodynamics. If it doesn't, it means it
has a leak" (quoted in Bourgi 2021). With this point, Saylor outines
the contours of an increasingly dominant ideological positionality
among Bitcoin enthusiasts—that Bitcoin's value, through proof-of-
work, is naturalized and secured through physics, namely, the laws
of thermodynamics (Mind/Matter 2021). Saylor's use of the term
"leak" proves instructive here, as it alludes to Bitcoin as a closed
(and therefore leakless) system because it "respects" the laws of
thermodynamics. This is a contradiction. The production of Bitcoin,
in this scenario, is the production of immutable certainty governed
by the natural laws of the universe. Proof-of-work relies on the
certainty of secure containment but, as we have seen with the
history of thermodynamics, certainty is rarely, if ever, certain. As
Prigogine (1997) reminds us, the entire history of thermodynamic
science is the move from cosmological reversability and certainty
to irreversibility and *uncertainty.* Leakage and loss are central to
this move. Proof-of-work advocates will rarely acknowledge these
leaks, but they are there, everywhere in the system. A blockchain,
as it happens, is a record of this leaking. Each hashed piece of data
directly corresponds to exhausted energy and the leaking of heat,

noise, labor, oil, and anything else that may escape containment
of the system. Where Michael Saylor sees a leakless system, I see
a system structured and defined by its profound leaking, a system
producing internal certainties through the production and valida-
tion of external uncertainties. It is leaking everywhere. I have the
oily syringe to prove it.

Thinking with Heat

We began this journey with an explosion, an uncontrollable
combustion of heat out from under a loose capacitor in a used
ASIC. Following this heat and its perilous escape took us through
an infrastructural analysis of proof-of-work, as well as a brief
history of thermodynamic science and its ideological positioning
at the center of the proof-of-work model. I focus on proof-of-work
not because it is a materially exceptional category of information
processing but rather because it is an ideological inversion of how
we normally consider digital information (Kirkwood 2021). This
inversion is revealing. As a computing practice, proof-of-work systems look a lot like other types of industrial-scale computing, with
server racks, wired ethernet connections, and massive energy bills.
But with their single-purpose use cases, and borderline-indexical
relationships between energy consumption and hashed data
outcomes, proof-of-work systems bring into relief entanglements
between energy, loss, and information more broadly. In this way,
heat, a systemic inevitability, becomes a heuristic for thinking
about computing from the outside in, through the eyes of the
already escaped, the already dissipated, the irrecoverably lost.

Thinking with heat and its relations is a "response-ability" (Haraway
2016) that can help us not only better attend to the materialities of
computing but also reframe our thinking to foreground that which
cannot be captured or contained by data in the first place—all
those often unintended outsides (Cooper 2021) that get boxed out
of our thinking about data relations. In addition to drawing attention to the labor, maintenance, and energy use on the outsides
of data infrastructures, thinking through heat to deal with these

processes of loss in information infrastructures can help bring energy humanities and discard studies to bear on broader issues of externality, uncertainty, and waste in big data and all that it fails to capture. A heat-centered energetic analysis necessarily begins from the point of failure, from the point where containment is breached, and as such brings into relief not just the data themselves but all that has been rendered as external, uncertain, and wasted in the process. It helps make visible the agential cuts (Barad 2007) and value judgments made by structures of power about what should and should not be included as data or their associated infrastructures. Big data's moribund traces and toxicities (Thylstrup 2019) reveal all sorts of undigestible, entropic subjects and spaces (Bridges 2021) deemed unuseful, unproductive, and unwanted. Heat can show us a way into and out of these spaces. Let us follow it.

Notes

1   I use the term *generate* (instead of *mine* or *mining*) because *generating* coins was the original term for this practice. This vernacular was dominant on both the P2P and BitcoinTalk forums from 2008 to late 2010, when the metaphor of *mining* began to supplant *generating.*

2   Cloud mining is a service that allows retail customers to lease machines owned and operated by a provider. Customers lease the right to generate cryptocurrency with these machines and pay fees to the hosting company.

References

Barad, Karen. 2007. *Meeting the Universe Halfway: Quantum Physics and the Entanglement of Matter and Meaning.* Durham. N.C.: Duke University Press.

Bateman, Tom. 2021. "Norway Could Back Bitcoin Mining Ban on Environmental Grounds." *Euronews,* November 17. https://www.euronews.com/next/2021/11/17/norway-could-back-european-bitcoin-mining-ban-as-minister-calls-energy-use-difficult-to-ju.

Bourgi, Sam. 2021. "Bitcoin Is a 'Masterpiece of Monetary Engineering' Michael Saylor Tells Austin Davis." *Cointelegraph,* February 10. https://cointelegraph.com/news/bitcoin-is-a-masterpiece-of-monetary-engineering-michael-saylor-tells-austin-davis.

Boyer, Dominic. 2018. "Infrastructure, Potential Energy, Revolution." In *The Promise of Infrastructure,* 223–43. Durham, N.C.: Duke University Press.

Bresson, Robert, dir. 1956. *A Man Escaped.* Gaumont.

Bridges, Lauren E. 2021. "Digital Failure: Unbecoming the 'Goog' Data Subject through

Entropic, Fugitive, and Queer Data." *Big Data and Society.* https://doi.org/10.1177
/2053951720977882.

Brunton, Finn. 2015. "Heat Exchanges." In *Moneylab Reader: An Intervention in Digital
Economy,* 159–72. Amsterdam: Institute of Network Cultures.

Brunton, Finn. 2019. *Digital Cash: The Unknown History of the Anarchists, Utopians, and
Technologists Who Created Cryptocurrency.* Princeton, N.J.: Princeton University
Press.

Clark, Nigel, and Kathryn Yusoff. 2014. "Combustion and Society: A Fire-Centered
History of Energy Use." *Theory, Culture, and Society* 31, no. 5: 203–26. https://doi
.org/10.1177/0263276414536929.

Cooper, Zane Griffin Talley. 2021. "Of Dog Kennels, Hard Drives and Magnets: Dealing
with Big Data Peripheries." *Big Data and Society.* https://doi.org/10.1177/20539517
211015430.

Cooper, Zane Griffin Talley, Katie Gressitt-Diaz, Kyle Cassidy, and Etienne Jacquot.
2019. *Alchemical Infrastructures: Making Blockchain in Iceland.* http://www.alchemi
calinfrastructures.com/.

Daggett, Cara New. 2019. *The Birth of Energy: Fossil Fuels, Thermodynamics, and the
Politics of Work.* Durham, N.C.: Duke University Press.

De Vries, Alex. 2021. "Bitcoin Energy Consumption Index." Digiconomist. https://digi
conomist.net/bitcoin-energy-consumption/.

Edwards, Paul. 1996. *The Closed World: Computers and the Politics of Discourse in Cold
War America.* Cambridge, Mass.: MIT Press.

Ensmenger, Nathan. 2018. "The Environmental History of Computing." *Technology and
Culture* 59, no. 4: S7–S33. https://doi.org/10.1353/tech.2018.0148.

Foster, John Bellamy, and Paul Burkett. 2016. *Marx and the Earth: An Anti-critique.*
Chicago: Haymarket Books.

Gridecon. 2010. "Bitcoin Minting Is Thermodynamically Perverse." Satoshi Nakamo-
to Institute. August 6. https://satoshi.nakamotoinstitute.org/posts/bitcointalk/
threads/167/.

Haraway, Donna J. 2016. *Staying with the Trouble: Making Kin in the Chthulucene.*
Durham, N.C.: Duke University Press.

Harney, Stefano, and Fred Moten. 2013. *The Undercommons: Fugitive Planning and
Black Study.* Wivenhoe, UK: Minor Compositions.

Hayles, N. Katherine. 1999. *How We Became Posthuman: Virtual Bodies in Cybernetics,
Literature, and Informatics.* Chicago: University of Chicago Press.

Hu, Tung-Hui. 2015. *A Prehistory of the Cloud.* Cambridge, Mass.: MIT Press.

Invest in Iceland. n.d. "Data Centers." https://www.invest.is/key-sectors/data-centers.

Johnson, Alix. 2019a. "Data Centers as Infrastructural In-Betweens: Expanding Connections and Enduring Marginalities in Iceland." *American Ethnologist* 46, no. 1:
75–88. https://doi.org/10.1111/amet.12735.

Johnson, Alix. 2019b. "Emplacing Data within Imperial Histories: Imagining Iceland
as Data Centers' 'Natural' Home." *Culture Machine.* https://culturemachine.net/
vol-18-the-nature-of-data-centers/emplacing-data/.

Khazraee, Moein, Luis Vega Gutierrez, Ikuo Magaki, and Michael Bedford Taylor.
2017. "Specializing a Planet's Computation: ASIC Clouds." *IEEE Micro* 37, no. 3:
62–69. https://doi.org/10.1109/MM.2017.49.

Kirkwood, Jeffrey West. 2021. "From Work to Proof of Work: Meaning and Value after Blockchain." *Critical Inquiry* 48, no. 2: 360–80. https://doi.org/10.1086/717303.

Kline, Ronald. 2015. *The Cybernetics Moment; or, Why We Call Our Age the Information Age.* Baltimore: Johns Hopkins University Press.

Klose, Alexander. 2015. *The Container Principle: How a Box Changes the Way We Think.* Cambridge, Mass.: MIT Press.

KPMG. 2018. *The Icelandic Data Center Industry.* Reykjavik: KMPG.

Kuhn, Thomas. 1996. *The Structure of Scientific Revolutions.* Chicago: University of Chicago Press.

Lally, Nick, Kelly Kay, and Jim Thatcher. 2019. "Computational Parasites and Hydropower: A Political Ecology of Bitcoin Mining on the Columbia River." *Environment and Planning E: Nature and Space* 5, no. 1. https://doi.org/10.1177/25148486198 67608.

Larkin, Brian. 2008. *Signal and Noise: Media, Infrastructure, and Urban Culture in Nigeria.* Durham, N.C.: Duke University Press.

Lepawsky, Josh. 2018. *Reassembling Rubbish: Worlding Electronic Waste.* Cambridge, Mass.: MIT Press.

Liboiron, Max, and Josh Lepawsky. 2022. *Discard Studies: Wasting, Systems, and Power.* Cambridge, Mass.: MIT Press.

Macy Conference. 2016. *Cybernetics—the Macy Conferences 1946–1953: The Complete Transactions.* Edited by C. Pias. First printing. Zurich: Diaphanes.

Magaki, Ikuo, Moein Khazraee, Luis Vega Gutierrez, and Michael Bedford Taylor. 2016. "ASIC Clouds: Specializing the Datacenter." In *2016 ACM/IEEE 43rd Annual International Symposium on Computer Architecture (ISCA),* 178–90. New York: IEEE. https://doi.org/10.1109/ISCA.2016.25.

Masanet, Erik, Arman Shehabi, Nuoa Lei, Sarah Smith, and Jonathan Koomey. 2020. "Recalibrating Global Data Center Energy-Use Estimates." *Science* 367, no. 6481: 984–86. https://doi.org/10.1126/science.aba3758.

Mattern, Shannon. 2021. *A City Is Not a Computer: Other Urban Intelligences.* Princeton, N.J.: Princeton University Press.

McKenzie, Jessica. 2021. "This Power Plant Stopped Burning Fossil Fuels. Then Bitcoin Came Along." *Grist,* May 6. https://grist.org/technology/bitcoin-greenidge-seneca -lake-cryptocurrency/.

Miller, Rich. 2014. "As Bitcoin Grows Mainstream, Data Center Provider Opportunity Widens." Data Center Knowledge. October 9. https://www.datacenterknowledge .com/archives/2014/10/09/amid-price-declines-bitcoin-miners-weigh-the-networks -future.

Mind/Matter. 2021. "Bitcoin's Monetary Superiority Is Guaranteed by Physics." *Bitcoin Magazine.* https://bitcoinmagazine.com/culture/bitcoin-monetary-superiority -physics.

Mora, Camilo, Randi Rollins, Katie Taladay, Michael Kantar, Mason Chock, Mio Shimada, and Erik Franklin. 2018. "Bitcoin Emissions Alone Could Push Global Warming above 2°C." *Nature Climate Change* 8, no. 11: 931–33. https://doi.org/10 .1038/s41558-018-0321-8.

Moro, Jeffrey. 2021. "Air-Conditioning the Internet: Data Center Securitization as Atmospheric Media." *Media Fields Journal,* April 26. http://mediafieldsjournal.org/

air-conditioning-the-internet/2021/4/26/air-conditioning-the-internet-data-center
-securitization-as.html.

Prigogine, Ilya. 1997. *The End of Certainty*. New York: Free Press.

Prigogine, Ilya, and Isabelle Stengers. 1984. *Order out of Chaos: Man's New Dialogue
with Nature*. New York: Verso.

Real Vision. 2021. "GreenBlocks: Green Energy Crypto Mining." https://www.real
vision.com/shows/the-interview-crypto/videos/greenblocks-green-energy-crypto
-mining/.

Richmond, Shane. 2018. "How the Blockchain Is Reshaping the Data Center." Verne
Global. May 4. https://web.archive.org/web/20200924150349/https://verneglobal
.com/news/blog/how-the-blockchain-is-reshaping-the-data-center.

Serres, Michel. 1982. *The Parasite*. Translated by Lawrence Schehr. Baltimore: Johns
Hopkins University Press.

Shannon, Claude, and Warren Weaver. 1949. *The Mathematical Theory of Communication*. Champaign: University of Illinois Press.

Shehabi, Arman, Sarah Smith, Dale Sartor, Richard Brown, Magnus Herrlin, Jonathan
Koomey, Eric Masanet, Nathaniel Horner, Ines Azevedo, and William Lintner.
2016. *United States Data Center Energy Usage Report*. LBNL-1005775, 1372902;
LBNL-1005775, 1372902. Washington, D.C.: U.S. Department of Energy. https://
doi.org/10.2172/1372902.

Smith, Crosbie. 1998. *The Science of Energy: A Cultural History of Energy Physics in Victorian Britain*. Chicago: University of Chicago Press.

Soluna. 2019. "FCAT Mining Summit—Future of Mining Panel Featuring John
Belizaire." YouTube video, 46:21, July 24. https://www.youtube.com/watch?v
=rMZhiGXVOMY.

Starosielski, Nicole. 2015. *The Undersea Network*. Durham, N.C.: Duke University Press.

Starosielski, Nicole. 2021. *Media Hot and Cold*. Durham, N.C.: Duke University Press.

Taffel, Sy. 2021. "Data and Oil: Metaphor, Materiality, and Metabolic Rifts." *New Media
and Society*. http://doi.org/10.1177/14614448211017887.

Taylor, Michael Bedford. 2017. "The Evolution of Bitcoin Hardware." *Computer* 50,
no. 9: 58–66. https://doi.org/10.1109/MC.2017.3571056.

Taylor, Michael Bedford, Luis Vega, Moein Khazraee, Ikuo Magaki, Scott Davidson,
and Dustin Richmond. 2020. "ASIC Clouds: Specializing the Datacenter for Planet-
Scale Applications." *Communications of the ACM* 63, no. 7: 103–9. https://dl.acm
.org/doi/10.1145/3399734.

Thylstrup, Nanna Bonde. 2019. "Data out of Place: Toxic Traces and the Politics of
Recycling." *Big Data and Society*. https://doi.org/10.1177/2053951719875479.

Tully, John. 2009. "A Victorian Ecological Disaster: Imperialism, the Telegraph, and
Gutta-Percha." *Journal of World History* 20, no. 4: 559–79.

Velkova, Julia. 2021. "Thermopolitics of Data: Cloud Infrastructures and Energy
Futures." *Cultural Studies* 35, no. 4–5: 663–83. https://doi.org/10.1080/09502386.2
021.1895243.

Wiener, Norbert. 1948. *Cybernetics; or, Control and Communication in the Animal and
the Machine*. Cambridge, Mass.: MIT Press.

[3]

Small Data: On Databases and Energy Infrastructures

Cindy Kaiying Lin

Indonesia's first Remote Sensing and Technology Data Center
is in the southern part of Jakarta, near Taman Mini Indonesia
Indah—a miniature park consisting of traditional life-sized homes
of Indonesia's ethnic groups, ancient monuments, and cable
cars to tour the state's vision of an "authentic" national identity.
Despite its proximity to a somewhat nationalistic project, a patchier
project for the people of Indonesia was being developed by two
government engineers. In the National Institute of Aeronautics and
Space's Remote Sensing and Technology Data Center, Rajah, one
of the developers of this project, greeted me at the center's office,
a distinctive building in a neighborhood with other government
and military buildings, a handful of smaller houses, and a famous
university. He was holding up a data server excitedly: "We finally
bought the servers!" Rajah was referring to data servers that he
would use for a government project—high-performance data
storage called LAPAN Engine to host an open access database of
remote sensing imagery data for provincial and regency governments to make maps and respond to disasters. "We have ordered
fourteen servers," Rajah repeated as I accompanied him to a highly
secure and temperature-regulated room. The approximately six

hundred square foot room was where Rajah stacked his server on a series of racks. "We are still waiting for the rest, but we have monitored and run speed tests on some of them."

Rajah conducted such tests because he wanted to know how much time was needed to transmit a satellite image from one PC to another. Indonesia's electric infrastructure is centralized and managed by the State Electricity Company. When the central grid is disrupted, power is immediately cut off. The energy supply is further exacerbated by poor electricity transmission lines and a lack of backup facilities (Pradana 2020). The centralization of energy is in part shaped by Dutch colonial patterns and concentration of power and wealth in urban Java Island, introducing and reifying the rural–urban divide in Indonesia (Setyawati 2022). The country also experiences slow internet connections, with less than 10 percent of Indonesia using a fixed broadband connection at home and office, leading to the poor maintenance of broadband internet network provision (Eloksari 2020). Given these energy constraints, Rajah insisted it was important to have their own data servers: "if we had signed up for Amazon Web Services, we would have to pay 2 to 3 billion rupiah a year [$143,000]. With 2 billion rupiah, I can get a lot of servers." Though Rajah didn't elaborate further, I suspected that LAPAN Engine also allowed him to tweak how quickly data could be transmitted across the island. Currently, operators are hired to download and send this imagery individually via WhatsApp or email to relevant authorities every morning. Such daily reports sometimes resulted in Rajah and his team of engineers being made responsible for delayed data reports. Rajah wanted to design a database that could give rural officials quick access to such data without having to rely solely on LAPAN.

Indonesia is the world's largest archipelago, with tropical rainforests, unrivaled biodiversity, and two of the world's largest islands—Borneo and New Guinea. It has also experienced some of the most devastating fires to its tropical peatlands in rural Indonesia. The engineering team at the National Institute of Aeronautics and

Space (in the Indonesian language, Lembaga Penerbangan dan Antariksa Nasional, or LAPAN) viewed distributing data to rural Indonesia as an effective but temporary solution for resolving fires. Members of LAPAN's engineering team believed that the efficient distribution of data could ensure that leaders throughout Indonesia could manage their own fires and, in turn, resolve the country's role in exacerbating the climate crisis.

This chapter analyzes how database arrangements by Indonesian engineers emphasize smallness in cloud computing, in contrast to the expansive scale and energy required to run large-scale data centers. Such emphasis on smallness not only pushes back against the contemporary use of cloud computing infrastructure to store and distribute data in ways that expend energy and water but also tells a different story of how database architectures are more than technical systems. My goal is to situate the design of cloud computing arrangements in relation to energy and labor—most importantly, energy, materialized in the form of a centralized electricity grid and intermittent network connection, has shaped the design of "small" databases for storing and distributing big data—and, subsequently, to how small databases, which were historically tied to the productivity of IT and computing programming labor, are expanded to encompass values of decentralization and autonomy in postcolonial Indonesia. Efficiency here, then, is not solely about the energy efficiency of the small database itself but also about reversing the script of labor productivity that has been tied to databases historically.

Efficiency, an industrial value, haunts data work in Indonesia today. Its most prominent advocate is Frederick Winson Taylor with his systems of scientific management. First developed at the turn of the twentieth century in the steel industry, the system of Taylorism instituted using specialized tools, breaking down tasks into measurable inputs and outputs, and introducing managerial authority to stimulate productivity (Alexander 2008, 12). Efficiency in Taylorism also meant the careful refinement and optimization of energy in relation between bodies and machines so that ever more work could be done. In earlier versions of databases, efficiency meant how quickly end users could query data on their own, freeing up the labor of programmers from database administration to develop computer applications. With the advent of cloud computing systems, clients can now rent servers from platform companies like Amazon and Google, instead of relying on programmers to maintain on-site data servers. Both configurations of databases universalize values of speed, stability, and labor productivity and celebrate images of technological innovation as new, expansive, and seamless. But database technologies rely on energy and network infrastructures, which do break down or become unreliable in Indonesia. When I refer to such conditions of infrastructural instability, I do not suggest that Indonesia is in a permanent condition of deficit. Rather, stating such conditions allows me to center how people like Rajah "fix and reinvent, reconfigure and reassemble into new combinations and new possibilities" for those involved (Jackson 2014, 222). Energy constraints and intermittent networks are hence not cases of exception but what David Nemer and Padma Chirumamilla (2019, 221) describe as the "backdrop in which the rhythms of everyday life must be forged."

My chapter recounts the building of a government-driven NoSQL ("Not only" Structured Query Language) database (which I use interchangeably with nonrelational databases) called LAPAN Engine that is today aimed at streaming data for disaster mitigation and fire mapping in Indonesia. The chapter borrows from twenty-one months of fieldwork in LAPAN with Indonesian computer scientists and remote sensing scientists. Although database design has historically been a site to optimize programmer productivity, it has served in Indonesia as an avenue for resiliency to be introduced into its design and challenged energy's fixation on growth, work, and expansion. In particular, I show how databases that have historically been used to maximize productivity are being adapted by Indonesian engineers to reverse social hierarchies in governance and reimagine a new way of storing big data that relies on energy infrastructures. Put simply, engagement with big data sometimes requires attending to its potential for smallness, that efficiency can be mobilized against management hierarchies, and that energy constraints can sometimes enrich, rather than limit, the autonomy of both engineers and Global South nations. The story of efficiency as told here intervenes in the inevitability of Western logics of energy that celebrate productive work and endorse resource extraction for imperial expansion.

How to Store Data?

A few afternoons after Rajah showed me his servers, operators received impatient WhatsApp messages from rural regency leaders requesting satellite images of potential fire locations. They needed to map fire locations on high-resolution satellite imagery to seek out emergency funds from the central government. LAPAN is legally instituted since 2016 to provide remote sensing and satellite imagery data to rural leaders for spatial planning purposes and map making. The fury of requests was challenged by the intermittent network that afternoon, with every operator's attempt to download images interrupted midway. That same afternoon, Rajah and Kamilah, the two computer engineers behind LAPAN Engine, brainstormed on how to make images small enough for operators to download. "You have to cut it in order to store it," Kamilah shared with us. Smallness here means dividing the big image into smaller units so that technical operators would not need to download data of large size. This not only freed up the labor of operators to do other things, Rajah and Kamilah were convinced, but also made the distribution of information faster.

In the last decade, organizations like LAPAN have designed databases that can deliver information with greater speed and reliability. To do this, one has to transform data—the practice of converting data from one format or structure into another format or structure—and pick the right database for such data. Here database design and data transformations are not only entities that consumed and transformed energy inputs; they also functioned as sites for optimizing programmers' labor practices. In the following paragraphs, I briefly introduce how LAPAN articulates NoSQL databases as sites for energy transformation and efficiency: to create a resilient database that can include end users as retrievers of information over low bandwidth and unstable electricity.

LAPAN Engine was a new challenge for the engineering team of two. As Rajah recounted to me, energy and internet constraints deter LAPAN from producing and distributing satellite remote sensing imagery data on demand. For instance, it sometimes takes more than an hour to download a LANDSAT scene that barely covers enough distance to make spatial plans for disaster evacuation. This also meant that operators waiting for LANDSAT data to be downloaded were "wasting" their time, unable to perform productive work.

To resolve this inefficiency in data download and retrieval, Rajah and Kamilah customized the LAPAN Engine to follow three principles. First, it would run on data that have been tiled. Tiling involves dividing or breaking down a satellite image into smaller-sized pieces encoded with certain values for quick retrieval from a database. Unlike text data, satellite imagery is unstructured data that need to be encoded with a certain value. It is also large in volume. A full coverage of Indonesia, for instance, requires 220 satellite snapshots—or what are technically known as satellite scenes. From a remote sensor, a full satellite image of Indonesia can total a minimum of 1,100 gigabytes—almost as large as 275 movie files.

Second, it was not only tiling that made data retrieval quick but the actual architecture of the database design, which I came to learn is nonhierarchical and resilient to breakdown. This resiliency is crucial so that data transmission can remain switched on, instead of experiencing frequent disruptions or outages. In other words, data transmission would not need to start from scratch if Indonesia were to experience a power outage or weak network signal, especially when data are being received in rural provinces where such situations are frequent.

This resiliency also meant that programmers like Rajah and Kamilah could finally make rural officials fully responsible for the work of disaster management and spatial planning, given that they could no longer excuse themselves based on poor bandwidth and electricity.

And finally, it is the ability of NoSQL database architecture to carry out simultaneous database transactions that Rajah and Kamilah were most concerned about: if they were to host a platform with multiple users, they wanted to make sure those users would be able to analyze data on the platform without any delay.

These three qualities of NoSQL database design—fast, resilient, and a platform for multiple users—suggest that through the tweaking of database design, LAPAN can become, in Rajah's words, "efficient" in disaster management. Rajah's emphasis on efficiency was particularly curious, given that alongside concerns around whether LAPAN's database design is sufficiently fast and can provide access for multiple users, there was an emphasis on resiliency—a value that is not commonly associated with energy infrastructures as documented by anthropologists of energy (e.g., Ferguson 1999; von Schnitzler 2016). In this way, Rajah showed me how efficiency had no universal value and possessed different meanings. How did data storage, then, come to be associated with industrial norms of efficiency like productivity and speed?[1] Put more simply, how did the quality of database design become evaluated on the basis of reducing idle time? What are the conditions in which data are understood to have to be stored, distributed, and shared with such deftness and stability? In what follows, I show how the story of efficiency in database design was initially tied to the ability to make (application) programmers[2] productive in the United States, making efficiency a characteristic built into early database design and its subsequent versions.

Designing a Database for End Users and Productivity

In the 1960s to 1970s, North American computer vendors, managers, and database designers, such as IBM, began to implement principles of efficiency into the design of digital databases—beginning with relational models. In 1969, former Royal Air Force pilot, University of Michigan communications science PhD holder, and IBM researcher Edgar Frank Codd wrote a paper, titled "A Relational Model of Data for Large Shared Databanks," that many computer science textbooks claimed as revolutionary in the history of information storage and retrieval. Codd proposed a new way of storing information in computers that he called the "relational database model" based on the mathematical theory of relations. First implemented in IBM's System R in the 1970s, relational models were celebrated for being "data independent"; that is, relational models allowed data to move across different application domains without "changes in storage structure and access strategy" (Chamberlin et al. 1981, 632). This particular feature resolved one of the long-standing problems of retrieving information: data storage can be separated from data retrieval. In other words, computer programmers are no longer in charge of solely storing and retrieving data.

New innovations in database design can be traced to the moment when computing hardware became less expensive. With the falling cost of hardware and the role of computing in larger projects, software has also witnessed developments in complexity and size since the 1960s (Ensmenger and Aspray 2002, 154). For instance, a group of Maryland researchers began to expand from using punched cards or linear records of tape to organizing their data in "tuples" to overcome hardware limitations. They named such organized data *multiplets.* Even though multiplets were not the same as the relational database system about which Codd wrote in 1969, they anticipated some of the basic properties of Codd's relational databases (Grier 2012). Multiplets allowed one to place data into a common unit without any bearing on how those data were actually stored in a database. More importantly, and in relation to Codd's tabular feature in relational databases, multiplets allowed one to organize data in ways that were easy to "manipulate with logical operations and easy to connect to larger classes of documents or information" (Miller et al. 1960). Multiplets' reach, however, was limited, as database companies emphasized building larger physical databases over transforming the design of these databases themselves.

At the same time, however, businesses began to view organizations as information processors. This started as early as the 1950s, when computers were used largely in industry spaces rather than for scientific applications. Famously, Hebert Simon (1957, 15), an American economist and information theorist, claimed that "information and advice flow in all directions through the organization." Peter Drucker (cited in Grier 2012, 13), an Austrian American management theorist whose writings were cited as inspirational to Microsoft's cofounder Bill Gates, wrote in 1957 that businesses have to "maintain the equilibrium between ends and means, output and effort." To do this, managers need to handle large amounts of information (Grier 2012). Databases, hence, became central to organizational labor practices, especially corporate attempts to harness managerial power and inform decision-making. According to a 1964 article in *Fortune,* "the power of the new so-called information technology is raising high management's power to make accurate decisions" (cited in Grier 2012, 14). Other corporate advisers anticipated that computers would be useful only if "we can ask them questions that matter. It is the task of management and science to help us to clarify these questions" (Gugerli 2012, 303). This quotation shows how databases became tied to managerial control, as touted by the corporate advisers who viewed the ability to manage information flows and balances as instrumental for organizational life.

As databases became integral to how organizations performed information query, and personal computers became ubiquitous in North America in the 1980s, computer programmers framed databases as a site for improving the productivity of technical experts. After introducing relational databases, Codd wrote in a 1982 *Communications of the ACM* article titled "Relational Database: A Practical Foundation for Productivity" how information can be stored and represented in ways that would improve the programmer's productivity and be used by end users, such as corporate advisers and managers (Codd [1982] 1989). Managers in the computing industry have long questioned the quality of programming since the 1950s. Historical studies of software labor show that in the United States, managers have complained about the lack of "quality" and experienced programmers and have encouraged programmers to certify themselves to demonstrate their performance since the 1960s (Ensmenger and Aspray 2002, 154). Codd's proposal that relational databases could improve programmers' productivity is hence one such step in further accrediting programmers and embracing the managerial vision of organizations as information processors.

For instance, Codd recounted how databases required programmers to navigate along access paths to reach the target data, making the labor required for such work enormous. For instance, any changes in the layout of the storage meant having to revise all programs and required too much manpower to maintain the application programs. Furthermore, the installation of these systems was too slow, and programmers faced a high learning curve to use these systems.

Codd listed out three objectives that relational databases could fulfill to increase information processing professionals' (or programmers') productivity. The first was *data independence*: the ability to distinguish between the logical and physical aspects of database management (including database design, data retrieval, and data manipulation). Simply put, this means one can change the base structure of the data without affecting the data required by users and programmers.

The second was a *communicability objective*: to make the model
structure simple so that programmers and end users have a shared
understanding of the data and can communicate with one another.
Codd's proposal of communicability was tied to IBM's invention
of the user-friendly query language Structured Query Language
(SQL), which allowed end users to type simple commands to query
databases, hence including nonprogrammer end users in the use
of relational databases (Date 1984, 9). For instance, when System
R became a major project for IBM, much emphasis was placed
on how end users responded to the system. The new emphasis
included not only the development of a search query language that
end users could pick up easily but also interface design that made
search "user-friendly." Although it is unclear whether "end users"
referred primarily to managers in organizations, literature on end
user computing in the 1980s focused largely on studying end user
groups in managerial, professional, and technical circles (Clement
1990). In the leading trade magazine about data processing,
Computer World, Joseph S. Mallory, a marketing representative and
systems engineer at IBM, wrote a 1982 article titled "The Rising
Tide of Information Management," in which he complimented SQL
as allowing "users with minimal training" to satisfy information
querying themselves, "freeing information systems staff to attend
to other tasks while employing the computer more effectively to
support management decision making" (87). Hence, productivity for
programmers is achieved when end users, ranging from managers
to system administrators, can query for information on their own
and hence "free" programmers from such labor.

The last objective was a *set-processing objective*: introducing high-
level language concepts to enable users to express operations
on large chunks of information, all at one time. These high-level
language concepts meant that one statement was sufficient for
processing multiple sets of records at a time. With these three
objectives, Codd ([1982] 1989, 116) proposed that relational databases could "simplify the task of developing application programs"
and allowed for easy "formulation of queries and updates to be

submitted from a terminal." It helped to free programmers from irrelevant concepts that forced them to code at a low level of detail, enabled programmers to synthesize a command for processing multiple data records simultaneously, and allowed end users to search databases themselves. Relational databases, in short, reduced programming time and included end users in the process of searching for and retrieving information.

Here efficiency was not only about manipulating the amount of time programmers took to store and retrieve data but also about including end users in the practice of information retrieval to improve an organization's functioning. At a time when personal computers and relational database systems became widely available across commercial industry, such as banking and aviation, the 1980s witnessed the integral role of databases in speeding up the productivity of IT and computing professionals. Put differently, what joins databases and the labor of programmers together is how energy as work can be transformed into a commodity form to be sold by end users, such as the managers of an organization.

Whereas the history of relational databases was all about making informational access easier and faster for a rapidly changing userbase in the context of the 1970s–1980s tech workforce, the development of NoSQL was the product of a different imperative: the need to maintain constant up-time for a consumer userbase. Today's computing industry often promotes NoSQL databases as efficient because of their ability to store big data, handle the increase in frequency of data access, and meet the needs of businesses interested in information search. The origin story of NoSQL starts with Dynamo, a data storage system developed by Amazon in 2004 to better handle its growing client database. Shortly after, one of the founders of Dynamo, Avinash Lakshman, developed a NoSQL database called Cassandra to meet Facebook's need to search inboxes on its platform (Lakshman and Malik 2010). In response to questions about how these platform companies could fulfill client demands with NoSQL databases, Lakshman replied in an interview in *Database Zone* magazine,

At Amazon, we had to build Dynamo to be multisite so it could survive a datacenter outage without causing downtime to Amazon.com, where downtime was directly correlated to *losses of millions of dollars.* Likewise, Cassandra was also built to be multisite to survive east or west coast datacenter outages at Facebook. Building resilient services is a higher priority than performance in today's always-on, connected world. I'm more likely to abandon a site or stop using a service if it incurs frequent outages than if it's a fraction of a second slower. (Smith 2017, emphasis added)

In this quotation, Lakshman prioritized a database's ability to maintain a resilient infrastructure over the speed of information retrieval to prevent the loss of revenue. Moving away from wasting time to fearing the loss of users, a different model of value creation was designed into NoSQL databases. Instead of processing inefficiencies, the concerns of developers who were designing such databases for North American tech companies were focused on lost time via sudden energy or network infrastructure disruptions. It was the illusion of the "always-on, connected world" across sites that Lakshman hoped to maintain by ensuring that breakdown frequencies were kept to a minimum. In addition, Lakshman claimed that programmers behind the database are not only database administrators storing data but also "part programmer, part automator, part infrastructure admin, and part database admin" (Smith 2017). These highly specialized roles packaged into one suggests that keeping a database infrastructure working is not only dependent on keeping database infrastructure efficient but also rests on the labor and multidisciplinary expertise of programmers who can *maintain* these databases. Efficiency here is not only about maximizing the input and output of energy through greater measurement and standardization of how programmers interact with code; it is also about databases ensuring a continuous flow of work and programmers embracing multiple roles at once. The nature of the work of database design and the stability of energy and network infrastructure have thus changed.

In both types of databases, efficiency is tied not only to programmer productivity but also to the ability of users to retrieve data in a short amount of time. Efficiency, in relational databases, however, focused on the ability to increase access to end users as well as improve programmer productivity. For nonrelational databases, on the other hand, the focus shifted to the stability of energy and internet network infrastructures such that any user—not only managers in corporations—could have access to information at a click. On one hand, efficiency actualized in relational database design made it possible for managers to organize their enterprises differently, especially through the interaction between database design, programmers, and even users. On the other hand, in nonrelational databases, the resiliency and stability of databases is an added quality to efficiency, allowing for information query and retrieval to happen around the clock, for all users, manager or not.

The ability to build resilient NoSQL database infrastructure, however, brings up an interesting question for an energy analytic more generally, given that (1) end users can now participate in the act of information query (2) with little to no disruption. Unlike North American tech corporations, whose focus is on generating revenue through maintaining a userbase, Rajah's (LAPAN engineer) notion of efficiency, undergirded by a need for a resilient database to overcome problems of energy and network constraints, serves a different purpose. In the next section, I show that though resilient databases became a way to paper over the structural problems of ill-maintained public infrastructure, such as electricity and internet broadband, they also allowed Indonesian engineers to imagine a new mode of data governance and infrastructure building.

Rural Officials as End Users: Reversing Master–Slave Architecture in Database Design

In the past decade, federal science agencies in the United States have contracted the services of tech corporations like Amazon to migrate data into cloud data servers. LAPAN, on the other hand, contrasted the convenience of subscribing to Big Tech cloud services versus developing their own database in-house. Kamilah elaborated, "We could have easily sent it to Google cloud, or have Amazon Web Services handle the data. At the very least, such storages allow us to provide consistent and reliable disaster-related information—one of the main roles of our institution." But both Rajah and Kamilah were instructed by senior officials in their institute not to work with North American tech companies like Google and Amazon because high-resolution satellite imagery contained sensitive information—mapping, especially national mapping, is a nationalistic enterprise. Senior officials recommended that Rajah contract a local Indonesian start-up to build it up quickly. But Rajah refused—he insisted that only the agency and the engineers who worked intimately with remote sensing data knew how such data should be formatted and how to make them as accessible as possible to rural users in Indonesia.

In keeping with the need to provide data with constraints such as low bandwidth and unstable electricity, Rajah and Kamilah had to ensure that their database did not break down. The first database the duo built broke down very quickly. They attributed this to what system builders call a single-point failure; that is, if one of the nodes (or documents in this document-store database called MongoDB) were to fail, due to faulty hardware, for instance, the whole web platform to stream satellite images would stop working. Rajah and Kamilah attributed this single-point failure to the legacy of master–slave architecture in MongoDB, where one database server (the master) sends data to be replicated to one or more other database servers (the slaves). Rajah and Kamilah understood MongoDB's master–slave architecture as inhibiting time-pressed retrieval of information on natural disasters. It also inhibited LAPAN from cultivating a more productive workforce.

Initially, LAPAN Engine was designed to reduce the time operators spent waiting for satellite imagery to be downloaded before moving on to their next task. Operators often took hours, if not days, to address requests for data ranging from processed imagery of fires to images of agriculture land. Disrupted electricity or internet connections meant that political leaders in Jakarta and rural Indonesia preferred that LAPAN send images through WhatsApp because its servers were viewed as more reliable than the country's own grid. Another common way to mitigate problems with infrastructure breakdown is for rural officials to travel personally to Jakarta to transfer data sets from LAPAN's data servers to a hard disk drive. Although initially, LAPAN viewed such problems of slowness as problems of productivity on the operators' end, it slowly learned that part of the problem with data accessibility was the centralization of national information in Jakarta.

Rajah and Kamilah believed that a different kind of database architecture had material implications for how they could facilitate user access to data sets. The ability to create a resilient infrastructure is especially important in this regard. To achieve resilience, they wanted to alter the database architecture itself so that users outside of Jakarta could easily retrieve information and would no longer have to rely solely on central government agencies like LAPAN for data access. They made an analogy between master–slave architecture and how information is transmitted in Indonesian governance: from Jakarta to rural provinces. Rajah elaborated, "This database reminds me of how we are treated as lower-level government workers—we have no ability to choose what we can do and how to do it. This makes us unable to provide information to everyone, even if the leaders of our country promise to do so. It also made it difficult for rural district and village officials who would like to access this data readily, but instead have to wait for operators to finish downloading such data or make a personal trip to Jakarta itself in order to store it in their own hard disk."

Rajah's wish to do away with the master–slave architecture in relational database design, I argue, cannot be read solely as an attempt to maximize operator productivity. When read against the architecture of the database itself, Rajah desired greater access for rural officials so that they could make prompt decisions based on

information, without having to rely on Jakarta as the main source
of information.

Consider how Rajah chose to work with Apache Cassandra, the free, open source NoSQL database that I described earlier. It is a database with a network that has no master nodes: the same data in a row can be replicated across several nodes. Its "masterless ring design" means that if one node is broken, the other nodes will continue operation. They believed that Cassandra could help mitigate the risk of data loss and poor access to information during Indonesia's regular electricity outages. The replication of data across different data nodes allowed Rajah and Kamilah to reimagine how data should be distributed without complete reliance on a single master node. This meant that these nodes were spread across different data centers, ensuring that if an on-site data server failed in rural Indonesia, a replica of the same row of data would be available in Jakarta. It also helped them resolve the slowness of bureaucratic decision-making in disaster management, given that the architecture ensured that users could always access an "always-on" architecture that would resist breakdown.

What is clear in all this is that database design was, for the first time in LAPAN, built also with an aspiration to transform bureaucratic hierarchy. It was through the properties of the database itself that creators felt a new social world was made possible: one without masters and slaves. This was crucial for Rajah because the role of providing information regarding disasters did not make for immediate decision-making around disaster prevention. In such time-pressed situations, efficiency is about more than guaranteeing speed—it is also about making sure that the databases remain on so that users can access the databases when they need them, wherever they are. As Rajah explained to me, "speed is efficiency. But speed relies on reliability. . . . Our users need to be able to use LAPAN Engine." For Rajah and Kamilah, the master–slave metaphor had actual material effects—it ensured that information storage and retrieval were not only centralized in Jakarta but possible to access from rural Indonesia based on Cassandra's database design.

Reversing the order and flow of information with the Cassandra database, LAPAN Engine had no masters and slaves. LAPAN Engine was an attempt to establish a peer-to-peer architecture in which everyone is the same to one another and everyone has an opportunity to be called upon. It also served as a direct intervention against the growing centralization of information in Jakarta and opened up different points of access and retrieval for rural leaders and governors.

For Small Data

Turning from the database design to the preparation of satellite image data themselves, I now show how Rajah and Kamilah worked with constraints to allow users to retrieve information quickly. Consider this: in using the masterless ring design of Cassandra, Rajah and Kamilah had already imposed a grid on a satellite scene. This grid made a series of tiles, each designated with a specific value. These values included the location where each tile could be found in a whole satellite scene and the date and time each tile was photographed.

Kamilah claimed that satellite imagery is the most difficult data to store. I asked why, curious as to what can make an image so difficult to keep. She replied that satellite images just contain too much information. Each pixel of satellite imagery can provide basic data ranging from brightness and the height of mountains to complex processed information like atmospheric quality, water pollution, and the presence of fire. Each pixel holds multiple kinds of information for which users will search to process and derive further insights. Hence, to make satellite image data easy to sort and search, Rajah and Kamilah needed to introduce structure to the data. This included tiling and naming each square a "satellite tile." Imposing a square grid makes the dense satellite imagery lighter and easier to search and retrieve over limited bandwidth and electricity flow. This means offering many smaller files rather than providing one large one. This data transformation was necessary if LAPAN wanted end users living in rural provinces, who experienced far greater infrastructure and energy constraints, to use LAPAN Engine.

Although most of LAPAN's users were rural leaders and ministerial officials in Indonesia, occasionally, researchers in academia and nongovernmental organizations across Asia requested satellite imagery from LAPAN. Rural leaders, however, are Rajah and Kamilah's main group of interest, because these leaders have direct access to on-the-ground disaster managers ranging from firefighters to local police. For instance, in my brief visit to South Sumatra, I encountered a firefighter who decided to use Google Earth and his own QGISS (free, open source mapping software) to develop fire maps to locate the nearest water fountain and deploy the necessary resources (manpower, vehicle) to the firefighting site. Rajah hoped to provide a similar service to the South Sumatran firefighter at a much higher resolution and with other necessary data sets that could aid in his operation. But to retrieve and stream several data sets on a web platform, Rajah and Kamilah needed to make big data small.

As Rajah saw it, and as Kamilah agreed at the time, they chose to tile satellite scenes because they knew that most Indonesian users do not have stable access to good WiFi and electricity. Downloading a whole satellite scene (one gigabyte) of a particular region, for instance, could take as long as thirty minutes if one had poor electricity or internet access. Indonesia ranks 118 out of 139 countries for its mobile internet speed, and electricity shortages can last as long as fifteen hours in the capital city of Jakarta. They needed to ensure that users could retrieve data in such an energy- and internet-constrained environment. By preparing data sets and designing a database that enabled users to locate certain tiles and, in turn, download specific areas of a satellite scene, Rajah and Kamilah hoped that provincial and regency officials would be able to access these data sets easily.

Furthermore, designing against energy and internet network

constraints, according to Kamilah, is a challenge unique to Indonesia and not met by "rich researchers who can compute as much as they want." The ability to retrieve data through tiles, or what I call small data, is a way Rajah and Kamilah hope to navigate such a challenge. Already, we have learned about the large emissions emitted when engineers from Big Tech companies and resource-rich universities store and run big data and machine learning models today. According to a recent article published by researchers concerned about the carbon footprint of tech, data centers will make up 45 percent of this footprint (up from 33 percent in 2010) and network infrastructure 24 percent (Dobbe and Whittaker 2019).

Here, cutting up images into smaller tiles and coding would ensure quick retrieval so that users could access data with as little electricity and bandwidth as possible. It would become, I suggest, a kind of low-carbon data infrastructure.

But senior officials in Rajah and Kamilah's workplace had other ideas. They saw it as a cost-efficient way to sell satellite images and earn a profit—not as long-term structural change for the Indonesian public in the form of equitable access to disaster information. These officials added that they could even sell customized data to users and earn a profit, given that LAPAN Engine could cater to more users and process them in ways that added value to information. What began as a means to increase mass access to environmental information morphed gradually into a market-based effort to secure competitive prices for satellite imagery.

An Alternative Energy Logic from Indonesia

In sum, I show how Rajah and Kamilah from LAPAN sought out a different kind of data infrastructure by developing a storage design that attended to resiliency and energy constraints. By insisting on the particularity of satellite imagery and the way such data can be stored and retrieved amid constant breakdown, Rajah and Kamilah showed how information access to rural officials can be decentralized. LAPAN Engine is an attempt at challenging the sole authority of central governments over satellite imagery by ensuring that rural district and village leaders could better obtain data directly, even if they faced energy constraints. Knowing that building such a database is possible also reassured Rajah and Kamilah, who could not rely on the cloud computing infrastructure of Google or Amazon. It retained the autonomy of public infrastructure, challenging the ubiquity of the public–private partnerships that now fund and build public-sector data infrastructures elsewhere. For instance, in the U.S. context, from 2007 to 2019, the Department of Homeland Security contracted and subcontracted services from American tech companies, with Amazon and Microsoft benefiting the most. Amazon saw a 400 percent increase in all federal contracts, and Microsoft 800 percent (Big Tech Sells War 2021). Most of these investments have been in military, intelligence, and law enforcement agencies. There is an urgent need for public and community-owned tech infrastructure, and LAPAN Engine offers a preview of one such alternative.

Furthermore, insisting on smallness also meant that Rajah and Kamilah provided alternate ways of storing and distributing information with mindfulness of the required bandwidth and electricity. They showed how designing for smallness in big data is also to imagine a different kind of knowledge infrastructure that does not enact what anthropologist Myles Lennon (2021) refers to as "a means of reduction" and a form of cost efficiency. A *means of reduction,* as Lennon defines it, is simply "apprehending a good or service solely in terms of its reductive capacities, enabling them to implement strategies to quantitatively reduce a negative phenomenon" (2).

I follow Lennon, then, by insisting on practices that not only resolve the harms of industrialized energy through reducing our energy consumption. If we are focused only on how our individual actions emit greenhouses gases, such as by cutting down our plastics use, we are focused on consumption. As my key interlocutors have shown, this only encourages senior officials to adopt a narrow way of thinking about how we can mitigate global climate change. It neglects that much of the energy used to power data centers today is manufactured in and extracted from the Global South, and much of the energy burden is on poor communities of color in the Global North.

We need to move away from a means of reduction to a means of production; that is, we need to look into the supply chain of energy needed to power our knowledge infrastructure today. I am not saying that focusing on reducing our carbon footprint is a bad strategy. Rather, my concern here is how we can create transnational solidarities in academic research by linking racial/environmental justice struggles at what Lennon (2021) call sites of energy consumption with racial/environmental justice struggles at sites of energy extraction and production in the Global South. These solidarities are mediated, I argue, through the design of databases today: the materiality of the database provides a lens through which we can better link prolific sites of energy consumption to prolific sites of energy extraction (for instance, by ensuring that small data can be downloaded in batches, one can begin to address the perils of extraction economies while at the same time providing access to users across the world). It is through database design that we can begin to pursue climate strategies that explicitly foreground questions of international environmental justice and move beyond a narrow preoccupation with reductions in carbon.

As I have shown in the case of Indonesia, engineers designed for a context where breakdown is a backdrop for continuity in everyday life. Rajah and Kamilah have designed a database that questions the historical determinacy of databases as inevitable tools for increasing programmer productivity and enacting managerial hierarchy, as they were once designed to do in North America. They showed how efficiency does not necessarily mean the conversion of energy inputs, such as electricity and programmers' labor, into rapid delivery of satellite images; efficiency is interpreted and implemented variedly in different energy and data cultures. In Indonesia, it is about creating a resilient infrastructure for rural leaders to govern and manage disasters within their own territories independently from central governance, rather than ensuring no downtime so that more users can populate on platforms like Amazon marketplace.

It is important to note here that producing small data did not, however, achieve progressive and radical change within LAPAN. In other words, there is no guarantee that transitioning to low-energy cultures would necessarily abolish our capitalist relations with the environment. As I have shown, superiors in LAPAN continue to insist on commercializing public data. It follows, then, that producing small data from the Global South is more than simply thrifting on electricity or improving operator productivity. It must also include understanding how relations of power can be inscribed into database design and who, as a result, has access to information within seemingly immaterial, nonhierarchical, and potentially green data relations.

Notes

I am thankful for the generosity of my interlocutors at Indonesia's National Institute of Aeronautics and Space. For funding that went into the research of this chapter, I acknowledge the Dow Sustainability Foundation at the University of Michigan and the Atkinson Center for Sustainability at Cornell University for their support.

1   Historians of technology have shown how efficiency is in and of itself a contradictory value, promoted to free humans from manual labor while at the same time exercising control over them (e.g., Alexander 2008; Daggett 2019).

2   I have placed "application" in parentheses, as from here onward, I refer to application programmers as programmers. However, typically, an application programmer is responsible for developing and maintaining application programs. For instance, such a programmer usually writes programs for specific tasks, such as programs to track inventory at a factory.

References

Alexander, Karns Jennifer. 2008. *The Mantra of Efficiency: From Waterwheel to Social Control.* Baltimore: Johns Hopkins University Press.
Big Tech Sells War. 2021. "About." https://bigtechsellswar.com/about/.

Chamberlin, Donald D., Morton M. Astrahan, Michael W. Blasgen, James N. Gray, W. Frank King, Bruce G. Lindsay, Raymond Lorie et al. 1981. "A History and Evaluation of System R." *Communications of the ACM* 24, no. 10: 632–46. https://doi .org/10.1145/358769.358784.

Clement, Andrew. 1990. "Cooperative Support for Computer Work: A Social Perspective on the Empowering of End Users." In *Proceedings of the 1990 ACM Conference on Computer-Supported Cooperative Work (CSCW '90),* 223–36. New York: Association for Computing Machinery. https://doi.org/10.1145/99332.99357.

Codd, Edgar Frank. 1983. "A Relational Model of Data for Large Shared Data Banks." *Communications of the ACM* 26, no. 1: 64–69. https://doi.org/10.1145/357980.35 8007.

Codd, Edgar Frank. (1982) 1989. "Relational Database: A Practical Foundation for Productivity." In *Readings in Artificial Intelligence and Databases,* 60–68. Burlington, Mass.: Morgan Kaufmann.

Daggett, Cara New. 2019. *The Birth of Energy: Fossil Fuels, Thermodynamics and the Politics of Work.* Durham, N.C.: Duke University Press.

Date, C. J. 1984. "A Critique of the SQL Database Language." *ACM SIGMOD Record* 14, no. 3: 8–54. https://doi.org/10.1145/984549.984551.

Dobbe, Roel, and Meredith Whittaker. 2019. "AI and Climate Change: How They're Connected, and What We Can Do about It." AI Now Institute. https://medium .com/@AINowInstitute/ai-and-climate-change-how-theyre-connected-and-what -we-can-do-about-it-6aa8d0f5b32c.

Eloksari, Eisya A. 2020. "Indonesian Internet Users Hit 196 Million, Still Concentrated in Java: APJII Survey." *Jakarta Post,* November 11. https://www.thejakartapost.com /news/2020/11/11/indonesian-internet-users-hit-196-million-still-concentrated -in-java-apjii-survey.html.

Ensmenger, Nathan, and William Aspray. 2002. "Software as Labor Process." In *History of Computing: Software Issues,* 139–65. Berlin: Springer.

Ferguson, James. 1999. *Expectations of Modernity: Myths and Meanings of Urban Life on the Zambian Copperbelt.* Berkeley: University of California Press.

Grier, David Alan. 2012. "The Relational Database and the Concept of the Information System." *IEEE Annals of the History of Computing* 34, no. 4: 9–17.

Gugerli, David. 2012. "The World as Database: On the Relation of Software Development, Query Methods, and Interpretative Independence." *Information and Culture* 47, no. 3: 288.

Jackson, Steven. 2014. "Rethinking Repair." In *Media Technologies: Essays on Communication, Materiality, and Society,* edited by Tarleton Gillespie, Pablo J. Boczkowski, and Kirsten A. Foot, 221–40. Cambridge, Mass.: MIT Press.

Lakshman, Avinash, and Prashant Malik. 2010. "Cassandra: A Decentralized Structured Storage System." *ACM SIGOPS Operating Systems Review* 44, no. 2: 35–40. https://doi.org/10.1145/1773912.1773922.

Lennon, Myles. 2021. "Energy Transitions in a Time of Intersecting Precarities: From Reductive Environmentalism to Antiracist Praxis." *Energy Research and Social Science* 73: 101930.

Mallory, Joseph S. 1982. "The Rising Tide of Information Management." *Computerworld* 16, no. 45.

Miller, L., J. Minker, W. G. Reed, and W. E. Shindle. 1960. "A Multi-level File Structure for Information Processing." Paper presented at the Western Joint IRE-AIEE-ACM Computer Conference. https://doi.org/10.1145/1460361.1460368.

Nemer, David, and Padma Chirumamilla. 2019. "Living in the Broken City: Infrastructural Inequity, Uncertainty, and the Materiality of the Digital in Brazil." In *DigitalSTS,* 221–39. Princeton, N.J.: Princeton University Press.

Pradana, Almo. 2020. "The Resilience of Indonesia's Electricity System." World Resource Institute, January 3. https://wri-indonesia.org/en/blog/resilience-indonesias-electricity-system.

Setyawati, Dinita. 2022. "Injustice and Environmental Harm in Extractive Industries and Solar Energy Policies in Indonesia." *International Journal for Crime, Justice, and Social Democracy* 11, no. 1: 14–27.

Simon, Hebert. 1957. *Administrative Behavior.* New York: *Free Press.*

Smith, Tom. 2017. "What's Next after Dynamo and Cassandra?" *Database Zone,* August 23. https://dzone.com/articles/whats-next-after-dynamo-and-cassandra.

von Schnitzler, Antina. 2016. *Democracy's Infrastructure: Techno-politics and Protest after Apartheid.* Princeton, N.J.: Princeton University Press.

Ambivalence and Intensity: On the Platform Energetics of NationBuilder

Jordan B. Kinder

> Canadian energy brings Indigenous communities from poverty to prosperity.
>
> —Canada Action
>
> It is time to build that pipeline.
>
> —Canada's Energy Citizens
>
> We must let governments at all levels know that we need pipeline approvals & construction, tidewater access.
>
> —Rally 4 Resources

These statements from a set of Canadian pro-oil groups and campaigns come up on a laptop screen in my office on the McGill University campus in Montréal, Québec. Montréal sits on unceded Indigenous territory, the caretakers of which are recognized as the Kanien'keha:ka or Mohawk nation. And these lands and waters have long served as a place of meeting and exchange for many Indigenous nations, including the Haudenosaunee and Anishinabeg. Some three kilometers from the flows of the St. Lawrence River, this space in which I sit is conditioned by industrial and postindustrial economies propelled by ongoing dispossession, particularly through the construction of hydroelectric megadams along the St. Lawrence and the establishment of a seaway over the course of the twentieth century. Once fueling electrified industrial relations, these dams now promise a so-called renewable base to a growing global tech sector that demands territory and energy for its infrastructures, especially data centers.

These geopolitical settings are linked to these groups and campaigns. All three are hosted on NationBuilder, a tech start-up that offers hard and soft web infrastructures to political campaigns, nonprofit advocacy organizations, and more.[1] For storing its data, NationBuilder itself relies on Amazon Web Services (AWS), which has a data center in greater Montréal. In this chapter, I detail the contours and consequences of these relationships between data and energy through an account of NationBuilder's political economies, ecologies, and imaginaries.

Data is the new oil. Or, at least, a set of provocative headlines over the past decade from media outlets such as *Wired, Forbes,* and the *Economist* would have us believe so.[2] Proclaiming this transition from an oil-driven society to a data-driven one rests on how the exchange values of both oil and data as raw materials fueling planetary economic relations are understood. But beyond equalizing data and oil as commodities fueling economies in overdetermined ways, a host of relationships come into view if this transformation is to be taken seriously—relationships between media and environment, between data and energy. And while economists and journalists debate whether data have truly displaced oil as the *ur*-commodity from which dominant social and ecological relations are mediated, fossil fuels continue to be burned. Electricity, integral to the digital media systems that allowed data to be thought of as the new oil, remains predominantly produced by coal across the globe, an energetic relation between data and energy whose consequences will be increasingly if unevenly felt in the near and far future.

This oil–data conjuncture highlights how the economic, material, and cultural conditions by which energy forms (here, fossil fuels) and objects of computation (here, data) relate to and shape one another. At data centers, energy and data meet in ways that make platforms possible. My employment of the platform concept is simultaneously expansive yet limiting. I follow definitions from critical perspectives in new media studies and the political economy of the digital present, such as those from political theorist Nick Srnicek (2017, 43), who understands platforms as "digital infrastructures that enable two or more groups to interact." In this view, platforms are important sites of cultural and economic mediation, and I follow Srnicek's hunch that "we can learn a lot about major tech companies by taking them to be economic actors within a capitalist mode of production" (3). Turning to platforms from this vantage point means examining the encounters between culture and economy as they meet at the platform in general and the data center in particular. These encounters are particularly significant given that, according to David B. Nieborg and Thomas Poell (2018, 4276), platforms are increasingly shaping both the internet and everyday life as the "platformization of cultural production" or "the penetration of economic, governmental and infrastructural extensions of digital platforms into the web and app ecosystems," taking hold at macro- and microscopic scales. As mediators of cultural, political, and economic exchange in the digital present— an infrastructural relation to be sure—platforms emerge as sites through which to address the material-energetic contours of the digital age and, as I show in this chapter, the energy systems and epistemologies that underwrite our digital present.

In this chapter, I propose "platform energetics" as a way of examining the interrelation between the material energy systems and relations on which digital media platforms rely and the energy imaginaries produced and circulated on these platforms. Taking methodological cues from recent work in the fields of media archaeology and environmental media studies that link the material-ecological tendencies or dispositions of digital media infrastructure to the social and cultural lives of energy systems and relations, platform energetics is a dialectical formation that centers the material-energetic lives of platforms as well as the energetic imaginaries mediated on them. In this way, platform energetics derives results from the energy analytic we described in this book's introduction and links closely to the larger digital energetics to which this book owes its name.

This chapter examines the platform energetics of one emergent, increasingly influential political engagement platform: NationBuilder. As I gesture to in the opening paragraph, NationBuilder is a tech start-up marketed to nonprofit organizations, political campaigns, and more. As communications scholars Fenwick McKelvey and Jill Piebiak (2018, 902) describe in perhaps the most thorough analysis of NationBuilder to date, NationBuilder provides "an on-demand, all-in-one solution: one platform to manage the campaign's email, website, voter database, donations, volunteer coordination, and communications." Since the early 2010s, the platform has played an instrumental, if controversial, role in many political campaigns, such as former president Donald Trump's successful 2016 run for the U.S. presidency. Just as increasingly, NationBuilder is also used for activist and nonprofit campaigns and organizations. My research studies the cultural politics of energy, infrastructure, media, and environment in what is now called Canada and, in particular, how Canadian oil has become a site of material and discursive struggle online and off (Kinder 2020). In doing this work over the past decade or so, I continue to encounter NationBuilder as a platform used by groups and organizations both in resistance to and in support of one of the most contentious industrial megaprojects in history and the site of much of my research—the tar sands. I focus on this field of conflict as a concentrated and exemplary site through which to develop the concept of platform energetics by examining how these competing energy imaginaries and epistemologies are realized through NationBuilder.

In its capacities as a data-driven political engagement platform, NationBuilder participates in the broader political economic phenomenon of what Nick Couldry and Ulises A. Mejias (2019) have recently termed "data colonialism." Data colonialism, as

Couldry and Mejias detail in *Costs of Connection: How Data Is Colonizing Human Life and Appropriating It for Capitalism,* describes an operation of contemporary capitalism in which social life becomes further commodified through the appropriation of data, ushering in what they identify as a new phase of capitalism that takes its cues from historical colonialism. Although the concept has received criticism, particularly from scholars of the Global South, I nevertheless see critical import in the concept of data colonialism.[3] This chapter puts the material, land-based relations of extractive energy systems that fuel data centers into conversation with data colonialism. These relations are refracted in competing energy imaginaries of the tar sands that take shape through ambivalence and intensity that fuel business as usual rather than challenge it. At stake in the ambivalence and intensity that underwrite Nation-Builder's platform energetics is the homogenization of activism and politics that foregrounds a bleak planetary future in ways that maintain and reproduce existing dominant extractive and settler-colonial relations.

On NationBuilder: A Platform Profile

"Run your nonprofit; Power your advocacy; Win your elections," urges the NationBuilder tagline. Founded in 2009 and based out of Los Angeles, California, NationBuilder began as an online tool for democratically generating policy proposals to be voted on by users. The tool was first implemented on a site called White House 2. As founder Jim Gilliam (2009) described the platform in the months leading up to its launch, NationBuilder "will be a general purpose operating system to run democracies online." To "run democracies online," White House 2 gathered real-world policy proposals alongside user-submitted ones that could be judged by users as a collective speculative exercise for "imagining how the White House might work if it was run completely democratically by thousands of people over the internet" (White House 2 2009). Those deemed worthy of implementation by users were endorsed with a click of a button; those deemed unworthy were opposed similarly. In this democratic purview, NationBuilder was initially developed as an open source platform whose source code was available as a public GitHub repository, an effort that modeled the platform's democratic ideals at the levels of form and content.

NationBuilder's early release aspired not only to mobilize the internet for democratic aims but for the internet itself to serve as a conduit for mediating change or, as a well-worn tagline from NationBuilder and the name of Gilliam's personal blog suggests, to "make the future." Consistent with a techno-utopian vision so prominent in the lofty ambitions of 1990s cyberculture, we continue to encounter these naive optimisms about the promise of the internet as an ideological hangover that has proven hard to remedy. This hangover persists despite ever-growing scholarship that details the pitfalls of these optimistic lines of sight. What might have read as a wide-eyed, aspirational optimism, however, now reads as characteristic industry hubris that is difficult to separate from a more insidious TechBro saviorism. It is perhaps unsurprising that Gilliam would publish a memoir in 2016 whose title captures this faith: *The Internet Is My Religion.*

Over a decade after its launch, NationBuilder has closed down and scaled out as it took on a format in friction with its early techno-utopian builds. This transition was an abrupt one, occurring sometime after Gilliam announced his vision for the platform in 2009 and its later early practical launch use-cases, such as Kathleen Wynne's successful 2012 run for Ontario premier. No longer publicly available on GitHub, the back-end operations of the platform were made opaque, with NationBuilder explicitly prohibiting attempts to copy or mirror the source code in its detailed "Acceptable Usage Policy" (NationBuilder 2018)—a move more in step with platform capitalism than platform democracy. NationBuilder transformed from an initiative to offer a kind of public architecture for doing democracy online and off to a platform made available to those willing and able to participate in a subscription-based model. Centralization and control became selling points, as McKelvey and Piebiak's (2018, 902) "all-in-one" characterization implies.

Yet, a residual idealism remains in the platform's branding and self-presentation. "We build the infrastructure for a world of creators by helping leaders develop and organize thriving communities," NationBuilder's (n.d.) mission statement reads. In this declaration of intent, infrastructure carries heavy semantic, symbolic, and epistemological weight when considered in the setting of platform energetics. Cultural theorist Lauren Berlant's work on infrastructure offers some clarity here. For Berlant (2016, 393), infrastructures are defined not only through their operation as the heavy material objects that undergird everyday life (think pipelines or data centers) but through the ways in which they make relations possible (think financial systems or digital platforms themselves). Infrastructures, then, are simultaneously the hard and soft materials and relations that are ultimately "defined by the movement or patterning of social form" (Berlant 2016, 393). In the domain of the soft resides "affective infrastructure" (Berlant 2016, 414), an influential term of Berlant's that carries with its use ambiguity across the humanities and social sciences (Bosworth 2022). Following Bosworth, and, I would suggest, Berlant, my usage of *infrastructure* names a relation more than a concrete thing—straddling the hard and the soft—of which affect forms a central pillar (Bosworth 2022). In the case of NationBuilder's self-presentation, invocations of infrastructure refer at once to both these hard and soft configurations that help establish and influence a variety of publics.

Where NationBuilder most explicitly provides the hard networked infrastructure necessary to power the communicative, public presentation of the platform's users, it also provides the soft through a universalized, generic form that users mobilize for ends ranging from winning an election to establishing a trade union's public presence. In my use of form here, I draw on intellectual traditions of political aesthetics that see form as that which shapes expectations of use as well as possibilities of use. Media theorist Caroline Levine (2015, 4–6) outlines five characteristics or tendencies of forms: forms constrain, forms differ, various forms overlap and intersect, forms travel, and forms do political work in particular historical contexts. And in their performance, forms operate according to affordances, "a term used to describe the potential uses or actions latent in materials and designs" (Levine 2015, 6). Turning to architectures of form and affordance here is to bring to the forefront how platforms shape and are shaped by both cultural imaginaries and material relations.

Corporate myth-making construes the NationBuilder platform as one through which its form mutually informs and shapes its content according to principles of a particular mode of digital democracy. Later sidestepping these more utopian originary visions, NationBuilder's product today is a platform that streamlines operations lifted primarily from grassroots activist and political campaign strategies and is made available to a base of subscribers regardless of the commitments and aims of those using the platform, save for some specific breaches of NationBuilder's "Acceptable Use Policy," such as inciting violence. Although invocations of Gilliam's original vision of a platform both fueled by and enacting democratic principles remain in its taglines and slogans, there is no doubt that NationBuilder today embodies platform capitalism, whose tenets are in friction with platform democracy, as it arguably strives for monopoly over campaigning and activism.

In doing research for this chapter, I attended a free, public online demonstration for prospective customers of NationBuilder. This demonstration walked through the key functions and features of the platform, which included lessons on how to parse through data gathered through registration and pledge forms with a particular focus on interpreting and mobilizing those data for strategic communicative ends, on one hand, and fundraising efforts, on the other. These two communicative and financial features form the foundational mechanics of NationBuilder. In terms of communication, users can mobilize the platform to send mass and targeted email blasts, filtering who receives a given email according to default and customizable tags, such as amounts donated, time volunteered, or location. The NationBuilder representative emphasized this feature, noting that the most financially dedicated users can be targeted for solicitation. Here, the communicative and financial operations of NationBuilder converge where parsing data allows for soliciting funds from a dedicated base.

It is telling that the representative of NationBuilder who ran the workshop I attended used a hypothetical political campaign as the default model to walk through when the platform's targeted customers include nonprofit advocacy organizations, trade unions, and more. Returning to the question of infrastructure's role in the form and function of platforms—the hard and the soft—these default settings are important to consider when meditating on platform energetics. Indeed, platforms like NationBuilder are made possible by those very same materials, economies, and relations that also make the internet as we know it possible. When I asked the representative of NationBuilder if data are hosted exclusively on U.S. servers, the rep's response was telling in these terms. The representative pointed out not only that data are stored on the cloud, which includes U.S. servers, but that data remain wholly owned by users themselves. NationBuilder, the representative clarified, does not access these data, and moreover, it follows the regional privacy laws in which the platform operates, including those of the European Union (EU), whose General Data Protection Regulation (GDPR) the EU considers to be "the toughest privacy and security law in the world" (GDPR 2018). Quite fairly, the representative interpreted my question as one concerned about data privacy. He geared most of his response to making clear that any data are the property of the client. But the unqualified cloud gestured to here imagines data in a dematerialized ether, as if there were no material, localized, land-based relations to those data. Rather than a question of privacy and security, although these are certainly prescient concerns, mine was a question that sought to clarify the territories on which the platform primarily held its data and, in turn, the energy systems and territorial relations to which Nation-Builder is bound.

On Data Centers and Data Colonialisms:
Platform Energetics beyond Metaphor

The cloud through which platforms like NationBuilder operate is not the immaterial space or site that has been presented to us as in Silicon Valley imaginaries. My interlocutor's appeal to the cloud as a means to succinctly, if vaguely, answer my question about where it is that NationBuilder's servers are located, however, underscores the purchase that such immaterial imaginaries continue to enjoy years after collective insistence on the materiality of the immaterial. Yet, the cloud, in my interlocutor's field of view, represented an unknowable, ethereal, and mysterious space out *there* rather than *here*. Of course, such ethereal cloud imaginaries abstract and obscure the host of hardware that props up the cloud from the microchip to the data center. Electricity fuels the broader cloud apparatus, for instance, while data centers and network cables demand land and territory, bound to energy systems and land and water use practices simultaneously capitalist and colonial in theory and practice.

Data, like oil and other fossil fuels when used as energy, are constituted in political economies and imaginaries as resources. And the logics that inform these resource relations are bound to historical material processes and relations of extractive capitalism. Teasing out these bound logics, processes, and relations as they collide at the platform offers a more materially oriented exposition of Couldry and Mejias's data colonialism, while putting pressure on some of the more universalizing claims about data and new colonial relations embedded in the concept. In his recent article on the material dimensions of the data–oil metaphor, media theorist Sy Taffel (2021, 13) instigates this work in conversation with Couldry and Mejias, drawing out the data–oil relation by revealing "how planetary-scale extractive industries are a prerequisite for the acquisition of digital data." Following Taffel, I turn from the data–oil conjuncture to more closely examine the land-based, territorial dimensions of the cloud as a way of further refining the concept of data colonialism.

Beyond their immediate relation to electricity, data are linked
to extractive and resource economies through what energy
historian Christopher F. Jones (2014, 9) has called "landscapes of
intensification." For Jones, landscapes of intensification are those
landscapes that are shaped in the service of energetic regimes of
industrial production through energy transmission that operate at
the expense of the rural peripheries for the urban centers—canals,
pipelines, and wires. To this formulation, we can add the data
center and other digital infrastructures.

NationBuilder, for instance, is imbricated in one of the largest cloud
infrastructural apparatuses on the planet: AWS. As Gilliam noted
in a 2011 blog post in response to the AWS blackout that rendered
about half of the web unusable for over a day, NationBuilder uses
Heroku, a third-party service hosted through AWS. This relationship
is confirmed today by a detailed list of NationBuilder's "subproces-
sors," which outlines the larger hard and soft infrastructures on
which the platform itself relies, including AWS for cloud services,
Stripe for financial ones, and Twilio, which provides application
programming interfaces for telecommunications, including SMS
services. In its reliance on AWS and a host of other platforms,
NationBuilder, like most platforms, is part of an unfolding and
intensifying planetary regime of energy, territory, and data that
platform energetics names.

A frontier of sorts has taken shape in the wake of these energetic
relations as tech companies look to favorable conditions for capital,
energy, and territory. Patrick Bresnihan and Patrick Brodie's (2021)
fieldwork in Ireland reveals how, in this pursuit of new territories
for operation, the division between rural and urban, town and
country, gets reinscribed on the data frontier, an extractive frontier
that in Ireland is underwritten by the "moebius strip of wind/data."
Even as renewable energy is pursued to fuel the cloud, these
same divisions so central to the transition to industrial capitalism
powered by fossil fuels (Malm 2016) are reproduced. This drama is
currently playing itself out as platform capital seeks new territories
on and through which to build the infrastructures of the digital

present in general and data centers in particular, all of which is conditioned by what Mél Hogan (2021) has termed the "data industrial complex."

In Canada, these favorable conditions, lubricated by ongoing settler colonialism, have brought the data frontier into contact with a historical one. Hydroelectricity providers like Hydro-Québec (n.d.) mobilize green discourses, for instance, to describe Québec as "home to clean clouds." AWS has fed into this imaginary as it operates a center in the metro Montréal region. But these centers operate in the shadow of colonial place-making. From the James Bay Hydro Project to the Beauharnois Generating Station, megadams in Québec have been sites of dispossession and displacement of Indigenous peoples. Over in Alberta, home of the tar sands, the abundance of liquefied natural gas was offered up in a throne speech by Alberta's United Conservative Party to further define Alberta as a "modern electricity powerhouse and a magnet for investment in emerging technology like data storage and cryptocurrency" (quoted in Stephenson 2022). Journalist Amanda Stephensen captures the spirit as old and new frontiers converge: "The oil-and-gas producing province that prides itself on its entre-preneurial history is now touting its ambition to become a North American hub for companies trading in and offering services relat-ed to Bitcoin, Ethereum, Dogecoin and other digital assets." Beyond metaphor, settler-colonial relations fuel the data center industrial complex and its adjacent initiatives like cryptocurrency. Here, the deepened impacts on land and territory cannot be overlooked as they operate as another site of ambivalence and intensity.

Bringing into view these territorial and energetic regimes of power as captured by platform energetics identifies limits to Couldry and Mejias's (2019) data colonialism. For Couldry and Mejias, data colonialism is a new process endemic to contemporary digital cap-italism. From the manufacturing of computing hardware in socially and ecologically damaging ways to the acquisition of territory for data centers, colonial relations fuel what Couldry and Mejias call the "Cloud Empire." In a brief passage early in their book, Couldry and Mejias account for these material relations and the ties between what they understand as historical colonialism and data colonialism. Citing the work of Lisa Parks and Nicole Starosielski, Couldry and Mejias describe how "the very infrastructure of digital networks . . . are the embodiment and medium of violence, the conduit through which extraction takes place" (45–46). Moreover, "the human and environmental relations of production also remain characteristically colonial" (46). For Couldry and Mejias, these material realities appear almost as footnotes to data colonialism, yet it is precisely these relations that the notion of platform energetics prioritizes in the first instance. Couldry and Mejias acknowledge the historical and material dynamics of the digital present that resemble historical and ongoing patterns of colonialism but arguably avoid fully incorporating these patterns into their delineation of data colonialism. Colonialism was and remains motivated by the acquisition of land in the first instance, the consequence of which is the dispossession of Indigenous peoples (Coulthard 2014). Data colonialism is no different.

What I propose in gentle friction with data colonialism's tendency to abstract is a way to account for the material-energetic relations of platform capitalism, particularly as dispossession and displacement remain foundational to old and new capitalisms. In the setting of NationBuilder's platform energetics, its ambivalence and intensity inflect how the platform gets mobilized by the architects and allies of Canada's fossil economy alongside those who seek to build a future beyond it. As data centers and other infrastructures that prop up the digital present contribute to ongoing processes of settler colonialism, so, too, does a cultural politics of energy that ultimately favors impasse rather than transition.

On Ambivalence: Between Ports and Forms

Little scholarship exists on NationBuilder, despite the platform playing key roles in recent major political events. In my encounters with NationBuilder through scholarly work on media and the cultural politics of Canadian oil, the platform appears only in

passing discussions of the larger campaign or efforts that mobilize
NationBuilder to their particular ends.[4] This underexamination
can be explained in part by the fact that, at the time of writing,
NationBuilder takes up little of the total market share in the
content management system (CMS) world. Far from the likes of
Squarespace, Wix, or WordPress—the three of which cumula-
tively run the back-end of over 37 percent of the top one million
websites—NationBuilder represents only 0.007 percent.[5] Whereas
the most popular CMS platforms, such as WordPress, appeal to a
more generic audience, NationBuilder targets a specific audience
of change makers. As my foregoing profile of the platform and my
experience with a walkthrough of the platform reveal, these change
makers are imagined to be (and likely *are*) political campaigns and
advocacy organizations—that is, actors whose primary aim is to
have real-world impacts in a broader political landscape. Despite
representing so little of the larger CMS market share, NationBuilder
arguably punches far above its weight.

McKelvey and Piebiak (2018) examine the mutual flows between
platforms and political practices through NationBuilder. Using
qualitative political communication methods and actor-network
theory to perform an analysis of Canadian users of NationBuilder,
McKelvey and Piebiak propose the term *porting* to describe the
"overall process of reciprocal influence and hybridization" of
platforms (903), for which NationBuilder serves as a pertinent case
study. Questions of form return. The vignette that opens McKelvey
and Piebiak's article is telling on these terms as they recount the
experience relayed to them by the campaign consultant company,
Groundforce Digital, responsible for the digital operations of
Wynne's successful 2012 run for Ontario premier. The ease through
which a campaign infrastructure could be put together from
scratch led a representative for Groundforce to exclaim, "Wow.
That is not normal" (quoted in McKelvey and Piebiak 2018, 902).

Porting operates with an ambivalence championed as a nonpartisan tendency. As I argue later in a closer look at how Nation-
Builder is mobilized to promote and challenge Canadian oil, the

ambivalence that underwrites porting ultimately favors already-dominant views and relations, including extractive relations with land and territory. As McKelvey and Piebiak (2018) detail, the ease through which NationBuilder provides an infrastructure for doing political and activist labor imposes a sort of template that defines what constitutes such labor. A significant consequence of this is a homogenization of campaigning and activism alongside its tethering to platform capitalism. Campaigns and activism become indistinguishable as platforms like NationBuilder shape what is possible and how, which is underwritten by data expansionism.

Where McKelvey and Piebiak "[follow] the actors" (Kriess, quoted in McKelvey and Piebiak 2018, 905), I extend this work by responding to Deborah Cowen's (2020, 471) call to "follow the infrastructure." As detailed in my earlier platform profile, NationBuilder is not only a medium for gathering data and making use of them but a kind of infrastructure upon which organizations and campaigns can be built. To this end, NationBuilder offers freely available crash courses on the steps to create a nonprofit organization, establish a web presence for an advocacy organization, or pursue a political campaign. In each case, NationBuilder offers a sort of streamlined algorithmic process that follows its corporate mantra—*build, power,* and *win.*

Despite these varied uses of the platform for differing ends, how NationBuilder perceives its users reveals a more centralized imagination of what it means to use the platform and act in the world through it. Customers are "Leaders." Subscribers and volunteers as categorized in the NationBuilder database are the "Nation," whereas the kinds of analytics used to quantify data are "Political Capital." McKelvey and Piebiak (2018) detail how the Nation serves as an organizational mechanism, while the tools that enable the tracking of Political Capital serve as mechanisms for communicative feedback to shape the contours of the Nation. If off-line, real-world democracy via digital democracy was once the aspiration of NationBuilder, these features reveal a limited imagination in how that future can be built. The foreclosure of how to *do* politics and activism embodied in NationBuilder's ambivalent form functions in tandem with the foreclosure of material-energetic futures as my rejoinders to the notion of data colonialism suggest—a platform energetics that operates through ambivalence that feeds intensity. This interplay between soft (i.e., creating and engaging publics) and hard (i.e., territorial and energetic) forms the crux of platform energetics.

On Intensity: Energy Imaginaries Collide at the Platform

In political and infrastructural terms, NationBuilder is an ambivalent platform by design. NationBuilder promises and delivers a replicable, portable generic form for users, regardless of aim and aspiration, to generate, manipulate, organize, access, and parse through data aggregated from a community of users. And these promises of realizing aspirations are made to a host of customers with varied and often oppositional aims as they hope to improve prospects to win their campaigns or more effectively support their causes through the use of NationBuilder. Ambivalence is not an unintended effect of the tendencies of platform relations but rather a selling point, as NationBuilder proudly declares that it is a nonpartisan enterprise at its core. But such nonpartisanship relies on a postpolitical understanding of the public sphere in which platforms operate and mediate. As we face intensifying conditions of inequality propelled by deepening climate change and dominant capitalist economic orders, is nonpartisanship even possible? And what does the future of activism look like when the formal characteristics of political campaigning and expression are shared among, for instance, those who seek to build a more socially and ecologically just future through the abolition of the fossil economy and those who want to sustain that economy?

These questions are pertinent in the context of NationBuilder's platform energetics, as these questions are enmeshed with the digital present's material-energetic intensities, whether or not such a conjuncture is at the forefront of users' attention. When the smoldering heat of the present demands the taking of sides (Malm 2018), in other words, what does it mean to use the disavowal of taking sides as a business model? How the tar sands are both promoted and challenged on NationBuilder points to an increasingly precarious condition where platforms—often seen as invisible in the infrastructural sense—mediate what kinds of politics and activisms are possible and, as a result, shape our potential futures in ways that are obscured by ambivalence.

In the United States and Canada, the tar sands represent one of the most contentious sites of resource extraction in recent history. As an emergent industrial megaproject, the tar sands were first made economically viable at scale in 1967, when the Great Canadian Oil Sands plant went online. The sands reside primarily across Treaty 8 territory in northern Alberta, imbricating the megaproject in historical and ongoing settler colonialism. The sands were first bestowed the signifier "tar" as a sensorial descriptor related to the better-known substance of tar; the raw bitumen that constitutes the sands is a sticky, tarlike substance, and settlers who gave it this name tapped into this more widely known substance (tar) to make this new one (bituminous sands) legible. Following the development of a resource-intensive process to separate the bitumen from the sands by chemist Dr. Karl Clark in the 1930s, the tar sands have grown rapidly into what energy historian Troy Vettese (2016) argues is "the largest single industrial project *ever*."

But since the mid- to late naughts, when a coalition of environmental and Indigenous nonprofits and activist groups came together to launch a coordinated campaign against the tar sands, tar has been figured primarily by proponents of the sands as a politically charged discursive assault on a neutral resource. One of these groups, a coalition of Indigenous and environmental organizations operating under the banner of the Dirty Oil Sands Network, mobilized "dirty" as a signifier to draw attention to the destructive social and ecological impacts that follow the extraction, upgrading, and transmission of tar sands oil (Kinder 2020, 171). In the wake of this campaign, which comprised a host of media, including books (e.g., Nikiforuk 2008) as well as documentary film (e.g., Iwerks 2009), the meaning and representation of Canadian oil was to be forever inflected by dirtiness. Here were the origins of a symbolic, representational struggle over signification of the tar sands as an abstracted resource that requires comparatively more resource inputs and produces more emissions in the process than conventional crude oil.

These struggles over signification have arguably moved from a more dispersed multimedia ecology to digital platforms, including social media most prominently. In the past decade or so, efforts by the architects and allies of Canada's fossil economy to challenge this dirty oil designation have taken shape and intensified. Where lobbying organizations like the Canadian Association of Petroleum Producers (CAPP) have used the dynamics of the contemporary web to garner public support, such as through its Canada's Energy Citizens (CEC) campaign, so have a series of oil advocacy groups distanced from industry, mirroring the kinds of campaigning and messaging that sought to disrupt the continued expansion of the tar sands. Self-described grassroots organizations and government campaigns have taken shape in this setting to establish what can now be understood more generally as a pro-oil movement whose links to far-right political and media ecologies cannot be understated. The movement was arguably kicked off in 2010 with the publication of a pro-oil manifesto penned by far-right media figure Ezra Levant. Titled *Ethical Oil: The Case for Canada's Oil Sands,* the book challenged arguments put forward by the dirty oil campaign, positing that owing to Canada's strong environmental regulations and status as one of the few liberal democracies that produces oil, tar sands oil is not dirty; it is ethical.

After *Ethical Oil,* throughout the 2010s, a series of groups have carried the torch, including Canada Action, CAPP's CEC, and Rally 4 Resources, which all take as their mandate a grassroots agenda to support the oil and gas industry, an industry with the most lobbying power in Canada next to banks (*Maclean's* 2013). As my opening lines point out, all three of these groups and campaigns use NationBuilder as their home page platform, linked to their broader social media presence on platforms like Facebook, Instagram, Twitter, and YouTube. Elsewhere, I have described this larger phenomenon as petroturfing (Kinder 2020), that is, a disingenuous framing and origin of this pro-oil project akin to Astroturfing. NationBuilder has played an underacknowledged role in legitimating the presentation and operation of these groups and organizations.

More recently, under the auspices of Alberta premier Jason Kenney's pet project the Energy War Room, NationBuilder has been mobilized for a state-sponsored initiative called Support Canadian Energy. The Energy War Room, officially called the Canadian Energy Centre, was established by Kenney to counter what his administration perceives as lies about the oil and gas industry (Heydari 2019). On the Support Canadian Energy site, visitors are invited to "take action" by signing pledges and petitions that take advantage of the affordances NationBuilder provides. These pledges include a call to "Stop the 'Just Transition,'" which asks visitors to fill out a form to send an email to the government of Canada, as well as a similar push to "Tell the Truth Netflix," which presents visitors with a form to send an email to Netflix Canada's head of communications. This campaign against Netflix was one of the initiative's first, as it charged a children's film hosted on Netflix with "spreading misinformation about the oil and gas industry" (Support Canadian Energy, n.d.).

In each of these use-cases, NationBuilder's form lends an aura of authenticity that benefits the broader pro-oil project. In form and function, the ease of use and implementation of NationBuilder underwrite a kind of authenticity through generic form where efforts to promote Canadian oil are made to be an equally valid political project as building a future beyond the fossil economy. More generally, the generic form offered by NationBuilder establishes an equalization of activist efforts, in which ambivalence leads to an

intensification of the material and symbolic conflicts and polarity
at the center of the oil culture wars in ways that end up stifling the
possibilities for disrupting the dominant fossil fuel energy regime.

Beyond these more direct activist efforts, political parties and
media organizations saturated in fossil fuels also rely on Nation-
Builder. Levant's own far-right media conglomerate *Rebel News,*
for instance, mobilizes the platform to host its articles and videos
while centralizing its social media and fundraising efforts. And the
new far-right Canadian political party the People's Party of Canada
also uses NationBuilder to maintain its campaigning presence. But
so, too, is NationBuilder used for progressive ends to challenge
Canada's fossil economy and its right-wing political apparatuses. An
Alberta-based alternative news outlet, the *Progress Report,* uses the
platform to publish articles, host its podcast, distribute a news-
letter, and more. It is precisely through this ambivalence where
the existing order is maintained as both fighting for change and
keeping things the same are pursued with NationBuilder.

Maintaining business as usual, in other words, becomes virtually
indistinguishable from attempts to build a future beyond fossil
and extractive capitalism. In the context of competing imaginaries
and epistemologies of how the tar sands are to be understood,
platform energetics brings into view how platforms intensify
extractive relations at material and symbolic levels. NationBuilder's
role in the oil culture wars details the critical purchase of platform
energetics, as the concept provides a framework to address the
mutually intensifying energetic base or infrastructural assemblages
of the platform economy and its superstructural relation to this
intensification through ambivalence. When ambivalence packaged
as balance or nonpartisanship becomes an end in itself in a
fundamentally unbalanced world marked by deepening climate
change and ongoing settler colonialism produced by the forces of
fossil and extractive capitalism, those who benefit from the existing
order will continue to do so.

Beyond the Ambivalence and Intensity of Platform Energetics

The social and ecological impacts of the infrastructures and energies of our cloud-based present have been and continue to be made visible by those of us working in the environmental humanities in general and environmental media studies in particular. These impacts coalesce at the data center where resources like water (Hogan 2015), heat (Velkova 2021; see also chapter 2), and electricity (Bresnihan and Brodie 2021) are managed or consumed in a political economy and ecology underwritten by extractivism and fossilized energy regimes. With the increasing platformization of cultural and political spheres, these, too, not only become embroiled in these patterns in determinant, material ways, but also in the ways that these spheres mediate energy imaginaries—our collective social, cultural, and affective relations to energy and how we understand those relations. Platform energetics clarifies these bound dynamics as it describes the material-ecological relations of platforms and the cultural imaginaries and affective relations surrounding energy sources that these platforms circulate and the kinds of energy politics they enable. What happens when idealized Silicon Valley visions of digital democracy, such as those put forward by NationBuilder, come into immediate friction with realities of ongoing dispossession in the form of a data colonialism that centers the politics of land and territory?

As questions of transition have served as animating critical inspiration in the energy and environmental humanities, media studies would do well to approach data relations in similar terms, as energy and platforms are historically bound. Energy futures and platform futures are intertwined. And although this chapter's goal has not been to provide solutions to the problem of mutually reinforcing regimes of platform, extractive, and fossil capitalism, but instead to initiate critical conversations in these terms through the notion of platform energetics, it is worth closing with a meditation on what shape some solutions might take.

Perhaps, as Cindy Kaiying Lin outlines in her account of Indonesian engineers that subvert the colonial forces of Big Tech's default solutions to database operations (chapter 3), the answer lies in regionally attuned practices that seek a more localized solution against a one-size-fits-all one that ends up further intensifying the stronghold of dominant platform energetics. Or, following theorists like Malm (2021), perhaps it involves undermining and disrupting infrastructures through targeted modes of nonviolent sabotage. The answer likely resides somewhere in a confluence of generative and destructive interventions that are animated by an alternative platform energetics, that is, a platform energetics beyond ambivalence and intensity.

Notes

I thank Anne, Cindy, and Zane for their sharp contributions and feedback in this collective exercise and Kees Schuller for editing chops, as well as Patrick Brodie for conversations that helped to refine some of the trajectories this chapter takes. Some of this chapter relies on research done in collaboration with Burç Köstem, Hannah Tollefson, and Ayesha Vemuri—I thank them for their comradeship. This research was made possible by funding from the Social Sciences and Humanities Research Council of Canada (SSHRC) and Fonds de recherche du Québec—société et culture (FRQSC).

1   As of June 2022, Canada's Energy Citizens has migrated from NationBuilder to WordPress.

2   Headlines include "Data Is the New Oil of the Digital Economy" (Yonego 2014) and "The World's Most Valuable Resource Is No Longer Oil, but Data" (*Economist* 2017).

3   These criticisms (e.g., Amrute and Murillo 2020, 3) point primarily to the imprecision of the concept and how it frames data and information technologies as inherently colonizing, which overlooks the "multiple roles that information technologies take across" the Global South. In my view, the pressure put on the concept of data colonialism in these ways carves out space to further refine its historical and material contours.

4   Communications scholar Patrick McCurdy (2019, 193, 197), for instance, very briefly meditates on the role of NationBuilder and data-driven politics in CAPP's CEC.

5   These figures were compiled from WhatCMS.org, a website that detects and ranks CMS platform usage across the internet (https://whatcms.org/). The percentage is determined by crawls and analysis of the top one million websites on the Internet. And while it may seem more appropriate to compare

NationBuilder with mass email and marketing platforms focused on relationships with users in the first instance, or customer relationship management (CRM) software like Mailchimp, it is the case that NationBuilder is more than a communication service, as some use it simply as a home page hosting platform to better integrate their home pages with social media. In other words, NationBuilder is simultaneously a CMS and a CRM and, indeed, is marketed as such.

References

Amrute, Sareeta, and Luis Felipe R. Murillo. 2020. "Introduction: Computing in/from the South." *Catalyst: Feminism, Theory, Technoscience* 6, no. 2: 1–23.

Berlant, Lauren. 2016. "The Commons: Infrastructures for Troubling Times." *Environment and Planning D: Society and Space* 34, no. 3: 393–419.

Bosworth, Kai. 2022. "What Is 'Affective Infrastructure'? Repairing an Underdefined Spatial Concept." *Dialogues in Human Geography.* https://doi.org/10.1177/204382 0622110702.

Bresnihan, Patrick, and Patrick Brodie. 2021. "New Extractive Frontiers in Ireland and the Moebius Strip of Wind/Data." *Environment and Planning E: Nature and Space* 4, no. 4: 1645–64.

Couldry, Nick, and Ulises A. Mejias. 2019. *The Costs of Connection: How Data Is Colonizing Human Life and Appropriating It for Capitalism.* Stanford, Calif.: Stanford University Press.

Coulthard, Glen Sean. 2014. *Red Skin, White Masks: Rejecting the Colonial Politics of Recognition.* Minneapolis: University of Minnesota Press.

Cowen, Deborah. 2020. "Following the Infrastructures of Empire: Notes on Cities, Settler Colonialism, and Method." *Urban Geography* 41, no. 4: 469–86.

Economist. 2017. "The World's Most Valuable Resource Is No Longer Oil, but Data." May 6. https://www.economist.com/leaders/2017/05/06/the-worlds-most-valuable -resource-is-no-longer-oil-but-data.

GDPR. 2018. "What Is GDPR, the EU's New Data Protection Law?" https://gdpr.eu/ what-is-gdpr/.

Gilliam, Jim. 2009. "Making the Future." *Make the Future,* April 11. https://web.archive .org/web/20101114000557/http://www.jimgilliam.com/2009/05/making-the-the -future/.

Gilliam, Jim. 2011. "Cloudy." *NationBuilder* (blog), April 22. https://nationbuilder.com/ cloudy.

Gilliam, Jim. 2016. *The Internet Is My Religion.* Los Angeles, Calif.: NationBuilder Books.

Heydari, Anis. 2019. "Jason Kenney Touts \$30M 'War Room' but Provides Few Details." *CBC News,* June 7. https://www.cbc.ca/news/canada/calgary/jason-kenney-war -room-calgary-1.5167205.

Hogan, Mél. 2015. "Data Flows and Water Woes: The Utah Data Center." *Big Data and Society* 2, no. 2: 1–12.

Hogan, Mél. 2021. "The Data Center Industrial Complex." In *Saturation: An Elemental*

Politics, edited by Melody Jue and Rafico Ruiz, 283–305. Durham, N.C.: Duke University Press.

Hydro-Québec. n.d. "Data Centers." https://www.hydroquebec.com/data-center/.

Iwerks, Leslie, dir. 2009. *Dirty Oil.* Canada.

Jones, Christopher F. 2014. *Routes of Power: Energy and Modern America.* Cambridge, Mass.: Harvard University Press.

Kinder, Jordan B. 2020. "From Dirty Oil to Ethical Oil: Petroturfing and the Cultural Politics of Canadian Oil after Social Media." *Journal of Environmental Media* 1, no. 2: 167–83.

Levant, Ezra. 2010. *Ethical Oil: The Case for Canada's Oil Sands.* Toronto: McClelland and Stewart.

Levine, Caroline. 2015. *Forms: Whole, Rhythm, Hierarchy, Network.* Princeton, N.J.: Princeton University Press.

Maclean's. 2013. "The Top Lobby Groups in Ottawa." December 5. https://www.mac leans.ca/news/canada/the-top-lobby-groups-in-ottawa/.

Malm, Andreas. 2016. *Fossil Capital: The Rise of Steam Power and the Roots of Global Warming.* New York: Verso.

Malm, Andreas. 2018. *The Progress of This Storm: Nature and Society in a Warming World.* New York: Verso.

Malm, Andreas. 2021. *How to Blow Up a Pipeline.* New York: Verso.

McCurdy, Patrick. 2019. "Fanning Flames of Discontent: A Case Study of Social Media, Populism, and Campaigning." In *Power Shift? Political Leadership and Social Media: Case Studies in Political Communication,* edited by David Taras and Richard Davis, 187–201. New York: Routledge.

McKelvey, Fenwick, and Jill Piebiak. 2018. "Porting the Political Campaign: The NationBuilder Platform and the Global Flows of Political Technology." *New Media and Society* 20, no. 3: 901–18.

NationBuilder. 2018. "3dna Corp. Acceptable Use Policy." https://nationbuilder.com/ acceptable_use.

NationBuilder. n.d. "About NationBuilder." https://nationbuilder.com/about.

Nieborg, David B., and Thomas Poell. 2018. "The Platformization of Cultural Production: Theorizing the Contingent Cultural Commodity." *New Media and Society* 20, no. 11: 4275–92.

Nikiforuk, Andrew. 2008. *Tar Sands: Dirty Oil and the Future of a Continent.* Vancouver: Greystone Books.

Srnicek, Nick. 2017. *Platform Capitalism.* Cambridge: Polity.

Stephenson, Amanda. 2022. "Alberta Sets Sights on Cryptocurrency 'Wild West,' Aims to Attract Maverick Companies." CTVNews Calgary, March 27. https://calgary .ctvnews.ca/alberta-sets-sights-on-cryptocurrency-wild-west-aims-to-attract -maverick-companies-1.5836593.

Support Canadian Energy. n.d. "Tell the Truth Netflix!" https://www.supportcanadian energy.ca/tell_the_truth_netflix.

Taffel, Sy. 2021. "Data and Oil: Metaphor, Materiality and Metabolic Rifts." *New Media and Society.* https://doi.org/10.1177/14614448211017887.

120   Velkova, Julia. 2021. "Thermopolitics of Data: Cloud Infrastructures and Energy Fu-
       tures." *Cultural Studies* 35, no. 4–5: 663–83.

Vettese, Troy. 2016. "At All Costs." *Jacobin,* July 13. https://jacobinmag.com/2016/07/
       alberta-wildfire-tar-sands-petroleum-energy-oil-crisis/.

White House 2. 2009. "White House 2: Where YOU Set the Nation's Priorities."
       September 3. https://web.archive.org/web/20090903053656/http://whitehouse
       2.org/.

Yonego, Joris Toonders. 2014. "Data Is the New Oil of the Digital Economy." *Wired,* July
       23. https://www.wired.com/insights/2014/07/data-new-oil-digital-economy/.

Authors

Zane Griffin Talley Cooper is a PhD candidate at the Annenberg School for Communication at the University of Pennsylvania and a doctoral fellow at the Center for Advanced Research on Global Communication.

Jordan B. Kinder (Métis) is a postdoctoral fellow in environmental humanities at the Mahindra Humanities Center, Harvard University (2022–23).

Cindy Kaiying Lin is an assistant professor in the College of Information Sciences and Technology at Pennsylvania State University.

Anne Pasek is an assistant professor and the Canada Research Chair in Media, Culture, and the Environment at Trent University.

Ingram Content Group UK Ltd.
Milton Keynes UK
UKHW031017140523
421698UK00016B/109

9 781517 915872